Gran Canaria
Travel Guide
Adventure

Discover Hidden Gems, Top Attractions, Relaxation Hotspots, Culinary Delights, and Up-to-Date Tips.

By

Christopher Morrell

COPYRIGHT NOTICE

This publication is copyright protected. This is only for personal use. No part of this publication may be, including but not limited to, reproduced, in any form or medium, stored in a data retrieval system or transmitted by or through any means, without prior written permission from the Author / Publisher.

Legal action will be pursued if this is breached.

DISCLAIMER

Please note that the information contained within this document is for educational purposes only. The information contained herein has been obtained from sources believed to be reliable at the time of publication. The opinions expressed herein are subject to change without notice.

Readers acknowledge that the Author / Publisher is not engaging in rendering legal, financial or professional advice. The Publisher / Author disclaims all warranties as to the accuracy, completeness, or adequacy of such information.

The Publisher assumes no liability for errors, omissions, or inadequacies in the information contained herein or from the interpretations thereof. The publisher / Author specifically disclaims any liability from the use or application of the information contained herein or from the interpretations thereof.

TABLE OF CONTENT

Introduction 10
Welcome to Gran Canaria 10
    Brief History 11
    Overview of Gran Canaria 12
    Why Visit Gran Canaria? 14

Chapter 1 19
How to Get to Gran Canaria 19
    By Air 19
    By Sea 20
    By Car 21
    Transportation Tips 22

Chapter 2 27
How to Get Around Gran Canaria 27
    Public Transportation 27
    Car Rentals 28
    Biking and Walking 30
    Tips for Navigating the Island 32

Chapter 3 35
Top Tourist Attractions 35
    Discover Historic Sites 35
    Explore Scenic Parks 36
    Visit Iconic Landmarks 37
    Uncover Hidden Gems 38

Chapter 4 40
Beaches of Gran Canaria 40
Overview of Beaches 40
Best Beaches for Relaxation 40
Top Spots for Water Activities 42
Hidden Coastal Treasures 45

Chapter 5 49
Experiencing Gran Canaria's Culture 49
Museums and Galleries 49
Festivals and Events 51
Local Cuisine and Dining 53
Traditional Music and Dance 55

Chapter 6 58
Outdoor Adventures in Gran Canaria 58
Hiking and Nature Trails 58
National and Natural Parks 61
Water Activities and Sports 63
Bird Watching 66

Chapter 7 71
Shopping in Gran Canaria 71
Local Markets 71
Shopping Streets 73
Souvenirs and Local Crafts 76

Chapter 8 80

Nightlife and Entertainment in Gran Canaria 80
- Bars and Pubs 80
- Nightclubs 81
- Live Music Venues 83
- Theatres and Cinemas 84

Chapter 9 88
What to Do and Not to Do in Gran Canaria 88
- Respecting Local Customs and Traditions 88
- Safety Tips 90
- Common Tourist Mistakes 92
- Responsible Tourism 93

Chapter 10 99
Itineraries and Sample Plans 99
- Weekend Getaway 99
- Cultural Immersion 102
- Outdoor Adventure 106
- Family-Friendly Trip 109
- Budget Travel 112

Chapter 11 118
Accommodation in Gran Canaria 118
- Overview of Accommodation Options 118
- Luxury Resorts 119
- Budget-Friendly Hotels 120
- Boutique Guesthouses 122
- Unique Stays 123

Chapter 12 127
Top Recommended Hotels and Resorts 127
    Best for Luxury 127
    Best for Budget 129
    Best for Families 130
    Best for Couples 132

Chapter 13 137
Choosing the Right Accommodation for You 137
    Factors to Consider 137
    Location and Amenities 139
    Reviews and Recommendations 142

Chapter 14 146
Booking Tips and Tricks 146
    Best Times to Book 146
    Finding Deals and Discounts 148
    Using Booking Platforms 150
    Practical Booking Tips 154

Chapter 15 158
Culinary Delights of Gran Canaria 158
    Must-Try Dishes 158
    Top Restaurants 160
    Cafés and Bakeries 162
    Tapas Bars 164

Chapter 16 168
Day Trips and Excursions in Gran Canaria 168

- Nearby Towns and Villages 168
- Natural Wonders 170
- Cultural Excursions 172

Chapter 17 180
When to Visit Gran Canaria 180
- Best Seasons and Weather 180
- Key Events and Festivals 182
- Off-Peak Travel Tips 184

Chapter 18 188
Health and Safety in Gran Canaria 188
- Essential Health Tips 188
- Staying Safe 190
- Emergency Contacts 193

Chapter 19 198
Language Tips for Travelers 198
- Basic Phrases 198
- Helpful Expressions 200
- Language Resources 201

Chapter 20 207
Sustainable and Responsible Tourism 207
- Eco-Friendly Practices 207
- Supporting Local Communities 209
- Minimizing Your Footprint 211

Appendix 215

Useful Contacts 215
Map of Gran Canaria 216
Map of Things to do in Gran Canaria 217
Glossary: Local Terms 218
Applications and Useful Resources 218
Addresses and Locations of Popular
Accommodations 219
Addresses and Locations of Popular Restaurants
and Cafés 219
Addresses and Locations of Popular Bars and
Clubs 220
Addresses and Locations of Top Attractions 221

Introduction

Welcome to Gran Canaria

Gran Canaria, a paradise where nature and culture come together to create an unforgettable experience. Nestled in the heart of the Canary Islands, this Spanish gem boasts a diverse array of attractions that cater to every type of traveler. Whether you're exploring the island for the first time or returning to uncover more of its treasures, this guidebook will be your ultimate companion, ensuring you have a fulfilling, fun, and enjoyable stay.

As you wander through Gran Canaria, you'll be greeted by a harmonious blend of breathtaking landscapes, vibrant towns, and serene beaches. The island embraces its rich history while continually evolving with new ideas and trends. It's a place where you can savor the simple pleasures of life, from enjoying tapas in a charming café to exploring the island's diverse ecosystems.

In the pages that follow, you'll discover the best that Gran Canaria has to offer. From its top tourist attractions and hidden gems to practical tips and detailed itineraries, this guidebook is designed to help you make the most of your visit. So, let's begin our journey through this enchanting island and see what makes Gran Canaria a must-visit destination.

Brief History

Gran Canaria's history is as rich and varied as the island itself. The island was originally inhabited by the Guanches, a native people who left behind a legacy of fascinating archaeological sites. In the 15th century, the Spanish conquered Gran Canaria, incorporating it into the Crown of Castile and marking the beginning of a new era.

Over the centuries, Gran Canaria evolved into a significant cultural and economic center, playing a pivotal role in the maritime trade routes between Europe, Africa, and the Americas. The island's strategic location made it a melting pot of cultures and a vital stopover for explorers and merchants.

In more recent history, Gran Canaria has become a popular tourist destination, known for its beautiful landscapes, welcoming climate, and vibrant culture. Today, the island continues to charm visitors with its unique blend of historical heritage and modern attractions.

Overview of Gran Canaria

Gran Canaria is an island that embodies the essence of Spanish hospitality and charm. With its striking landscapes, lively towns, and rich cultural scene, Gran Canaria promises to captivate and inspire. The island's compact size makes it easy to explore by car, bus, or bike, allowing you to fully immerse yourself in its unique atmosphere.

The heart of Gran Canaria is Las Palmas, a bustling city that serves as the island's main gathering place. Here, you'll find outdoor cafés, the historic district of Vegueta, and the elegant Las Canteras Beach, whose golden sands and clear waters stand as a testament to the island's natural beauty.

Just a short drive from Las Palmas is the stunning landscape of the central mountains, where you can wander through pine forests, marvel at volcanic formations, and enjoy panoramic views of the island. This area is home to some of Gran Canaria's most important landmarks, including Roque Nublo, a towering volcanic rock that is one of the island's most iconic symbols.

Gran Canaria is also renowned for its diverse natural parks, offering plenty of opportunities for outdoor adventures. The Maspalomas Dunes, located along the southern coast, provide a surreal desert landscape with rolling sand dunes and picturesque beaches. The nearby Palmitos Park, with its lush gardens and exotic wildlife, is perfect for those seeking a bit of adventure and discovery.

For those interested in contemporary culture, the island offers a vibrant arts scene with numerous festivals and events throughout the year. The Alfredo Kraus Auditorium and the Cueva Pintada Museum are highlights, offering a fascinating exploration of art and history.

Gran Canaria's location in the Atlantic Ocean means that beautiful beaches and water-based activities are just a short distance away. Whether you're looking to take a leisurely boat cruise, go scuba diving, or simply enjoy a seaside picnic, the ocean adds a serene charm to the island.

Why Visit Gran Canaria?

Why should Gran Canaria be at the top of your travel list? Here are just a few reasons why this captivating island deserves your attention:

1. Rich Cultural Heritage: Gran Canaria's history is woven into the very fabric of the island. From its ancient Guanche roots to its role in maritime trade, the island is a living museum that offers a glimpse into centuries of art, architecture, and culture.

2. Vibrant Arts Scene: Gran Canaria celebrates creativity and innovation. The island hosts numerous festivals and events throughout the year, including the Carnival of Las Palmas and the Canary Islands Music Festival. Art lovers will also appreciate the island's many galleries and

museums, such as the CAAM (Atlantic Center of Modern Art).

3. Culinary Delights: Gran Canaria's food scene is a delightful fusion of traditional and contemporary flavors. The island's markets are brimming with fresh, local produce, and its restaurants offer everything from classic Spanish cuisine to innovative fusion dishes. Be sure to try local specialties like papas arrugadas (wrinkled potatoes) and mojo sauce.

4. Beautiful Beaches: With its location in the Atlantic Ocean, Gran Canaria is the perfect base for exploring beautiful beaches and engaging in water-based activities. Whether you prefer a scenic boat ride or a leisurely beach day, you'll find plenty of options for enjoying the island's natural beauty.

5. Outdoor Adventures: For those who love the great outdoors, Gran Canaria offers a wealth of opportunities for hiking, cycling, and exploring nature. The central mountains and their extensive network of trails are a paradise for nature enthusiasts, with stunning rock formations and scenic walking routes.

6. Family-Friendly Fun: Gran Canaria is a great destination for families, with plenty of activities and attractions to keep kids entertained. The island's parks and gardens provide ample space for outdoor play, while attractions like the Sioux City Park and the Poema del Mar Aquarium offer educational and fun experiences for all ages.

7. Shopping and Nightlife: Gran Canaria's shopping scene is a mix of high-end boutiques, charming markets, and quirky shops. The island's nightlife is equally diverse, with everything from cozy wine bars and lively pubs to trendy nightclubs and live music venues. Whatever your style, you'll find plenty of options for a fun night out.

8. Warm and Welcoming Locals: One of the highlights of visiting Gran Canaria is the warmth and friendliness of its residents. The locals are proud of their island and are always happy to share their knowledge and recommendations with visitors. Don't be shy about striking up a conversation and asking for tips – you're sure to receive a warm welcome.

9. Ease of Access: Gran Canaria is well-connected by air and sea, making it an easy destination to reach. The island's modern transportation system makes

it simple to get around, whether you're exploring the vibrant towns or venturing out to the stunning countryside.

10. Sustainable Tourism: Gran Canaria is committed to sustainable tourism practices, with numerous initiatives aimed at preserving the island's natural and cultural heritage. From eco-friendly accommodations to local food markets, the island offers plenty of ways to enjoy a responsible and environmentally friendly visit.

With all these amazing attributes, it's no wonder that Gran Canaria is a favorite destination for travelers from around the world. This guidebook will take you through every aspect of the island, providing detailed information and insider tips to help you make the most of your stay.

In the chapters ahead, you'll find everything you need to plan your trip, from practical advice on getting around and choosing the right accommodation to in-depth guides to the island's top attractions and hidden gems. We've also included itineraries tailored to different types of travelers, whether you're here for a quick weekend getaway, a cultural immersion, an outdoor adventure, a family-friendly trip, or a budget-friendly vacation.

Gran Canaria is an island that has something for everyone, and we're excited to help you discover all that it has to offer. So, let's begin our journey through this captivating island. Turn the page and get ready to explore the beauty, history, and excitement that await you in Gran Canaria. Welcome to Gran Canaria – your adventure starts here!

Chapter 1

How to Get to Gran Canaria

By Air

Ah, the thrill of flying! Touching down on Gran Canaria is always exciting. If you're planning your trip, flying is probably the most convenient option. The island's main airport, Gran Canaria Airport (LPA), is well-connected to major cities across Europe and beyond. It's just 18 kilometers south of the capital, Las Palmas, making it a central hub for travelers.

I remember my first flight to Gran Canaria – I flew from Madrid with Iberia, and the journey was smooth and pleasant. The flight took about 2.5 hours, and I was captivated by the view as we approached the island. The rugged coastlines and blue waters were a sight to behold from the plane window.

Several airlines operate flights to Gran Canaria. If you're coming from the UK, you can catch a direct flight with British Airways, easyJet, or Ryanair. Prices vary, but you can find round-trip tickets ranging from €100 to €300, depending on the season and how far in advance you book.

Once you land, the airport is well-equipped with amenities. There are plenty of shops, cafes, and car rental services. If you need assistance, the information desk is very helpful. I recommend grabbing a coffee at Cafe Ritazza while you wait for your luggage – their pastries are delightful.

By Sea

If you're up for a more adventurous start to your holiday, arriving by sea is an option. Ferries connect Gran Canaria to other Canary Islands and the Spanish mainland. The main port is Puerto de la Luz in Las Palmas, a bustling hub that's always a flurry of activity.

I took a ferry from Tenerife once, and it was an incredible experience. The journey took about 2.5 hours with Fred Olsen Express, and I spent most of the time on the deck, soaking in the sea breeze and the beautiful vistas. The ferry ride itself was comfortable, with plenty of seating, a cafe, and even a small shop.

From the Spanish mainland, you can catch a ferry from Cádiz. This journey is much longer, around 36 hours, but it's a fantastic way to see the Atlantic Ocean. Naviera Armas and Trasmediterránea are the two main operators, and they offer cabin accommodations if you prefer to travel overnight. Prices for these ferries range from €60 to €120 per person.

Upon arriving at Puerto de la Luz, the first thing you'll notice is the impressive skyline of Las Palmas. The port area is vibrant, with plenty of places to grab a bite or do some shopping before heading to your final destination. Don't miss the chance to visit the nearby Castillo de la Luz, a historic fortress that offers a glimpse into the island's past.

By Car

Driving to Gran Canaria isn't an option unless you're already on one of the Canary Islands, but once you're here, renting a car is an excellent way to explore. The island is well-connected by a network of roads that are easy to navigate, even for first-timers.

During one of my trips, I rented a car from Cicar at the airport. The process was straightforward, and the staff was incredibly friendly. I opted for a small hatchback, perfect for the narrow roads in some of the smaller villages. Prices for car rentals vary, but you can expect to pay around €20-€50 per day, depending on the vehicle type and season.

Driving around Gran Canaria is a joy. The GC-1 highway runs along the eastern coast, connecting Las Palmas in the north to Puerto de Mogán in the south. The scenery along this route is stunning – picture-perfect beaches, rugged cliffs, and lush greenery. Just be sure to carry some cash for the occasional toll road.

Transportation Tips

Navigating transportation options in Gran Canaria can be a bit overwhelming at first, but here are a few tips from my personal experiences to help you out:

1. Booking Flights: Try to book your flights as early as possible. Prices tend to spike closer to the travel dates,

especially during peak tourist seasons (December to February and June to August). I once snagged a fantastic deal on a round-trip ticket by booking six months in advance.

2. Ferry Reservations: If you're taking a ferry, it's wise to book your tickets online beforehand. I learned this the hard way when I showed up at the port in Tenerife only to find the ferry fully booked. Most ferry companies have user-friendly websites where you can check schedules and make reservations.

3. Car Rentals: Always compare prices from different rental companies. Websites like Rentalcars.com can be handy for this. Also, don't forget to check the insurance policy – I've had friends who were caught off guard by additional fees for damages not covered by basic insurance.

4. Public Transportation: Gran Canaria has an efficient public bus system operated by Global. It's affordable and covers most tourist spots. A bus ride from the airport to Las Palmas costs around €2.95. Buses are clean and punctual, but during peak hours, they can get crowded.

5. Local Taxis: Taxis are readily available, and they're relatively inexpensive. For instance, a taxi ride from

the airport to Las Palmas costs around €30. Always ensure the meter is running to avoid any surprises. The taxi drivers are generally friendly and helpful – I had one driver who gave me an impromptu tour of the city en route to my hotel!

6. Cycling and Walking: If you're staying in Las Palmas or any of the coastal towns, cycling and walking are fantastic ways to get around. Many areas have dedicated bike lanes, and the weather is usually perfect for a stroll. I spent countless afternoons walking along the promenade in Las Palmas, enjoying the ocean views.

7. Language Barrier: While many people in the tourist industry speak English, knowing a few basic Spanish phrases can be very helpful, especially in more remote areas. On one of my trips, my limited Spanish made a huge difference when asking for directions in a small mountain village.

8. Currency and Payments: Gran Canaria uses the Euro (€). Credit and debit cards are widely accepted, but it's a good idea to carry some cash, especially for small purchases in markets or rural areas. ATMs are plentiful, and I've never had any trouble withdrawing money.

9. Safety: Gran Canaria is generally very safe for tourists. However, like any popular destination, it's wise to stay vigilant. Keep an eye on your belongings, especially in crowded areas. I've always felt safe here, even when walking alone at night.

10. Local Etiquette: Spaniards are known for their warm hospitality, and Gran Canaria is no exception. A friendly "Hola" or "Buenos días" goes a long way. When dining out, it's customary to leave a small tip, around 5-10%, for good service.

By air, by sea, or by car, getting to and around Gran Canaria is part of the adventure. Each method offers its unique experiences and perspectives of this beautiful island. Whether you're gazing at the coastline from a plane, feeling the ocean breeze on a ferry, or driving through scenic routes, the journey to Gran Canaria is sure to be as memorable as the destination itself.

Gran Canaria Airport (LPA)

Address: Autopista GC-1, km 16, 35230, Las Palmas, Spain

Phone: +34 928 579 000

Fred Olsen Express

Address: Muelle de La Luz, s/n, 35008 Las Palmas de Gran Canaria, Las Palmas, Spain

Phone: +34 902 100 107

Cicar Car Rental

Address: Gran Canaria Airport, Autopista GC-1, km 16, 35230, Las Palmas, Spain

Phone: +34 928 822 900

Naviera Armas

Address: Estación Marítima, s/n, 35008 Las Palmas de Gran Canaria, Las Palmas, Spain

Phone: +34 902 456 500

Remember, the best way to enjoy Gran Canaria is to immerse yourself fully in the journey. Take your time, enjoy the sights, and make memories that will last a lifetime.

Chapter 2

How to Get Around Gran Canaria

Public Transportation

When I first arrived in Gran Canaria, I was pleasantly surprised by the efficiency and convenience of the public transportation system. The island's bus service, known as Global, covers a vast network, making it easy to get around without needing a car. The buses are modern, clean, and well-maintained, offering a comfortable ride whether you're heading to the beach or exploring the mountainous interior.

One of my favorite routes is the number 30, which travels from the bustling capital of Las Palmas de Gran Canaria to the popular resort town of Maspalomas. It's a scenic journey that offers a glimpse of the island's diverse landscapes. The buses run frequently, and the fares are quite reasonable, usually around €2-€5 depending on the distance. You can purchase tickets directly from the driver, but I recommend getting a BONO card, which offers discounted fares and can be recharged as needed.

Another tip: the bus stations in major towns like Las Palmas and Maspalomas have helpful information desks where you can get schedules and route maps. Don't hesitate to ask the friendly staff for assistance; they're always willing to help.

Contact Information:

Global Bus Services, Las Palmas de Gran Canaria Bus Station

Address: Estación de Guaguas de San Telmo, Calle León y Castillo, 18, 35003 Las Palmas de Gran Canaria, Las Palmas, Spain

Phone: +34 928 252 630

Car Rentals

For those who prefer the freedom of exploring at their own pace, renting a car in Gran Canaria is a fantastic option. I remember the thrill of hitting the open road and discovering hidden gems that aren't easily accessible by public transport. The island's roads are generally in excellent condition, and the stunning coastal drives are an adventure in themselves.

There are numerous car rental agencies, both international chains and local companies, with competitive prices. During my stay, I rented a car from Cicar, a well-known local company with a reputation for excellent service. They offered a wide range of vehicles, from compact cars to luxury SUVs, and their rates were quite reasonable – I paid about €30 per day for a compact car.

Driving around Gran Canaria is relatively straightforward. The major highways, such as the GC-1 and GC-2, are well-marked and connect the main towns and cities. However, be prepared for some narrow, winding roads, especially when venturing into the mountainous regions. It's all part of the adventure, and the breathtaking views are worth it!

Contact Information:

Cicar Car Rentals

Address: Aeropuerto de Gran Canaria, 35230, Las Palmas, Spain

Phone: +34 928 822 900

Pro Tip: Always check if your accommodation offers free parking, as it can save you time and money. Also, keep an eye out for petrol stations, especially in rural areas where they can be sparse.

Biking and Walking

Gran Canaria is a paradise for cyclists and walkers alike. I vividly recall the sense of freedom and connection with nature while biking along the scenic coastal paths and hiking through lush forests. Whether you're an avid cyclist or just enjoy a leisurely walk, the island offers something for everyone.

The bike rental scene in Gran Canaria is booming, with numerous shops offering high-quality bikes for rent. I rented a bike from Free Motion in Playa del

Inglés, a popular choice among both tourists and locals. They provide a wide range of bikes, from mountain bikes to e-bikes, and their rates are quite reasonable, starting at around €15 per day. The staff were incredibly helpful, providing maps and tips on the best routes.

For those who prefer walking, Gran Canaria boasts an extensive network of well-marked trails. One of my favorite hikes was through the Tamadaba Natural Park, where the trails weave through dense pine forests and offer stunning views of the coastline. Another memorable walk was along the Paseo de Las Canteras in Las Palmas, a vibrant promenade lined with cafés and shops, perfect for a leisurely stroll.

Contact Information:

Free Motion Bike Center

Address: Avenida de Italia, 12, 35100 Playa del Inglés, Las Palmas, Spain

Phone: +34 928 777 777

Pro Tip: Wear comfortable shoes and carry plenty of water, especially during the summer months when temperatures can soar. Also, always follow marked trails and respect the natural environment.

Tips for Navigating the Island

Navigating Gran Canaria is relatively easy, but there are a few tips and tricks I picked up that can make your experience even smoother.

1. Download Offline Maps: Mobile coverage is generally good, but there are some remote areas where signal can be spotty. Downloading offline maps on Google Maps or another navigation app can be a lifesaver.

2. Learn Some Basic Spanish Phrases: While many locals speak English, knowing a few basic Spanish phrases can go a long way in making your interactions smoother and more enjoyable. Simple phrases like "Por favor" (please), "Gracias" (thank you), and "¿Dónde está…?" (where is…) can be very helpful.

3. Respect Local Customs: Gran Canaria is a place with rich cultural traditions. When visiting religious sites or small villages, dress modestly and be mindful

of local customs. It's a sign of respect that the locals deeply appreciate.

4. Stay Hydrated: The island's climate can be quite warm, especially during the summer. Always carry a bottle of water with you, whether you're hiking, biking, or just exploring the town.

5. Use Sun Protection: The sun in Gran Canaria can be very strong. Don't forget to apply sunscreen, wear a hat, and use sunglasses to protect yourself from UV rays.

6. Parking Tips: In busy tourist areas, parking can sometimes be a challenge. Look for designated parking lots or areas where parking is allowed. Avoid parking in restricted zones to prevent fines.

7. Emergency Numbers: It's always good to know the local emergency numbers. In Spain, the general emergency number is 112, which connects you to police, fire, and medical services.

8. Local Help: Don't hesitate to ask locals for directions or recommendations. The people of Gran Canaria are incredibly friendly and willing to help. I had some of my best experiences following the advice of locals.

Navigating Gran Canaria was a delightful experience, made even better by the friendly locals and the stunning scenery at every turn. Whether you choose to explore by bus, car, bike, or on foot, each mode of transportation offers a unique perspective of this beautiful island. Enjoy every moment, and don't forget to take in the breathtaking views along the way!

Contact Information:

Gran Canaria Tourist Office

Address: Calle Mayor de Triana, 93, 35002 Las Palmas de Gran Canaria, Las Palmas, Spain

Phone: +34 928 219 600

Pro Tip: Plan your routes and activities in advance, but also leave some room for spontaneous adventures. Gran Canaria is full of surprises, and sometimes the best experiences come from the unexpected.

Chapter 3

Top Tourist Attractions

Discover Historic Sites

One of the most enriching experiences in Gran Canaria is exploring its historic sites. I remember my first visit to Vegueta, the old town of Las Palmas. Walking through the cobblestone streets felt like stepping back in time. Vegueta is home to the impressive Santa Ana Cathedral (Plaza de Santa Ana, 35001 Las Palmas de Gran Canaria), which dates back to the 15th century. The architecture is a blend of Gothic and Neoclassical styles, and the views from the bell tower are breathtaking. It costs around €3 to enter, and it's worth every cent for the panoramic views alone. You can contact them at +34 928 317 840 for more information.

Nearby, the Casa de Colón (Calle Colón, 1, 35001 Las Palmas de Gran Canaria) is another gem. This museum is dedicated to Christopher Columbus, who reportedly stayed here during his voyages. The museum provides fascinating insights into the history of the Canary Islands and their connection to the New World. The entrance fee is €4, and you can reach them at +34 928 312 373.

Explore Scenic Parks

Gran Canaria's natural beauty is undeniable, and its parks are perfect for immersing oneself in the island's diverse landscapes. One of my favorites is Palmitos Park (Barranco de Los Palmitos, s/n, 35109 Maspalomas), a botanical garden and aviary nestled in a lush valley. The park features a stunning array of tropical plants and exotic birds. I vividly remember the bird of prey show; watching eagles and hawks soar above was mesmerizing. The park is open daily from 10 AM to 6 PM, and the entrance fee is €33 for adults and €24 for children. For more details, you can call +34 928 797 070.

Another beautiful spot is Parque Doramas (Calle León y Castillo, 227, 35005 Las Palmas de Gran Canaria). This park is a verdant oasis in the heart of the city, with beautifully landscaped gardens, fountains, and playgrounds. It's a fantastic place to relax and take in the local flora. I often found myself here with a good book, enjoying the serene atmosphere. There's no entrance fee, and it's a perfect spot for a peaceful afternoon.

Visit Iconic Landmarks

Gran Canaria is dotted with iconic landmarks that capture the essence of the island. One such landmark is Roque Nublo, a volcanic rock formation that stands at 1,813 meters above sea level. The hike to Roque Nublo is moderately challenging but incredibly rewarding. I recall the sense of accomplishment I felt reaching the summit, where the views were absolutely stunning. The trailhead is located near La Goleta, and it's best to start early in the day to avoid the midday heat. There's no entrance fee, and it's a must-visit for any hiking enthusiast.

Another must-see is the Maspalomas Dunes (Playa del Inglés, 35100 Maspalomas). This natural reserve is a spectacular desert landscape right next to the ocean. Walking through the dunes feels like being in the Sahara, with the golden sands stretching as far as the eye can see. The area is also home to a beautiful beach and a lighthouse, which adds to the picturesque setting. It's a perfect spot for a leisurely walk or a day at the beach. Again, there's no entrance fee, but I recommend bringing plenty of water and sunscreen.

Uncover Hidden Gems

Beyond the well-trodden paths, Gran Canaria has numerous hidden gems waiting to be discovered. One such place is the Cueva Pintada Museum and Archaeological Park (Calle Audiencia, 2, 35460 Gáldar). This site offers a fascinating glimpse into the pre-Hispanic history of the Canary Islands. The museum is built around a series of ancient cave paintings that were discovered in the 19th century. The guided tours are excellent, providing detailed explanations of the island's indigenous culture. The entrance fee is €6, and you can contact them at +34 928 895 746 for more information.

Another lesser-known spot is the charming village of Tejeda. Nestled in the mountains, Tejeda is often described as one of the most beautiful villages in Spain. The views from the village are simply breathtaking, with the surrounding peaks and valleys creating a stunning backdrop. While in Tejeda, I highly recommend visiting the Museo de la Historia y

Tradiciones (Calle Párroco Rodriguez Vega, 2, 35360 Tejeda). This small museum offers a fascinating look at the local history and traditions. The entrance fee is €3, and it's well worth it.

Gran Canaria also boasts some beautiful and less crowded beaches. One of my personal favorites is Playa de Güigüi, which can only be reached by a challenging hike or boat. The effort is well worth it, as the beach is a tranquil paradise with crystal-clear waters and pristine sands. There are no facilities here, so bring everything you need for a day of relaxation.

Exploring Gran Canaria's top tourist attractions has been an unforgettable experience. From historic sites and scenic parks to iconic landmarks and hidden gems, the island offers a diverse array of experiences for every traveler. Whether you're here for the first time or returning for another visit, Gran Canaria's rich history, natural beauty, and cultural treasures will leave you with lasting memories.

Chapter 4

Beaches of Gran Canaria

Overview of Beaches

Gran Canaria is an island that seems almost custom-built for beach lovers. With its warm climate, golden sands, and turquoise waters, it's no wonder that visitors from around the world flock here to enjoy the sun, sea, and sand. Having spent a good amount of time exploring the island, I can tell you that each beach has its own unique charm, catering to different tastes and activities. Whether you're looking for a lively beach with lots of amenities or a secluded spot for some peace and quiet, Gran Canaria has it all.

Best Beaches for Relaxation

When it comes to unwinding and soaking up the sun, there are a few beaches that stand out as particularly ideal for relaxation.

Playa de Maspalomas

One of my personal favorites for a relaxing day is Playa de Maspalomas. Located near the famous Maspalomas Dunes, this beach offers a stunning backdrop of golden sands stretching as far as the eye can see. The beach is spacious, so even during peak times, you can find a quiet spot to lay down your towel. I remember one lazy afternoon just lying there, the sound of the waves gently lapping at the shore, a gentle breeze keeping the heat at bay. It's truly a slice of paradise.

You can rent a sunbed and umbrella for around €10 per day, which is perfect if you plan to stay for several hours. There are also plenty of beachside bars and restaurants where you can grab a refreshing drink or a bite to eat. If you're into people-watching, this is the place to be. The beach attracts a diverse crowd, from families to solo travelers, each enjoying the tranquil setting.

Playa de Amadores

Another excellent beach for relaxation is Playa de Amadores. This beach is a man-made marvel, designed with relaxation in mind. The crescent-shaped bay, calm waters, and soft, white sand create a perfect environment for lounging. I particularly love coming here in the late afternoon when the sun starts to dip, casting a golden glow over everything. The beach has a serene atmosphere, and the water is usually calm, making it ideal for a relaxing swim.

There are numerous restaurants and cafes along the promenade, offering everything from local dishes to international cuisine. You can rent a sunbed and umbrella here as well, typically for about €12 for the day. One of my favorite spots is the Blue Beach Club (Avenida del Amparo, s/n, 35130 Amadores), where you can enjoy a cocktail while taking in the stunning views.

Top Spots for Water Activities

Gran Canaria isn't just about lying on the beach; it's also a fantastic destination for water sports enthusiasts. Whether you're into surfing, diving, or something a bit more unique, there's plenty to keep you entertained.

Playa de Las Canteras

For those who love to stay active, Playa de Las Canteras in Las Palmas is a must-visit. This beach is often referred to as one of the best urban beaches in Europe, and for good reason. The long stretch of golden sand is perfect for a morning jog, but it's the water activities that really shine here.

The beach is protected by a natural reef, La Barra, which makes the waters calm and ideal for snorkeling and swimming. On my last visit, I spent hours snorkeling just off the shore, marveling at the vibrant marine life. There are several shops along the promenade where you can rent equipment or book a diving excursion. If you're new to diving, I highly recommend Buceo Canarias (Calle Tenerife, 4, 35008 Las Palmas de Gran Canaria, +34 928 26 36 17), where the friendly instructors will guide you through your first underwater adventure.

Playa de Pozo Izquierdo

For windsurfing and kitesurfing, Playa de Pozo Izquierdo is the go-to spot. Located on the eastern coast of the island, this beach is famous for its strong winds and waves, making it a haven for water sports enthusiasts. Every year, it hosts the Gran Canaria Wind and Waves Festival, attracting top surfers from around the globe.

I remember my first time trying windsurfing here; the adrenaline rush was incredible. There are several schools along the beach where you can take lessons or rent equipment. One of the best is Cutre Windsurf Center (Avenida del Muelle, 11, 35100 Pozo Izquierdo, +34 928 79 16 18). They offer courses for all levels, and their instructors are both knowledgeable and encouraging.

Playa de Puerto Rico

If you're looking for a bit of everything, head to Playa de Puerto Rico. This beach is nestled in a sheltered bay, making the waters calm and perfect for a variety of activities. You can rent jet skis, go parasailing, or try out a banana boat ride. On a recent visit, I tried jet skiing for the first time, and it was an absolute blast. The feeling of speeding across the water with the wind in my hair is something I'll never forget.

The beach is lined with shops and kiosks offering rentals and excursions. I recommend booking a boat trip with Spirit of the Sea (Calle Puerto Base, 1, 35130 Puerto Rico de Gran Canaria, +34 928 56 11 04). They offer dolphin and whale watching tours, which are a fantastic way to experience the marine life around Gran Canaria.

Hidden Coastal Treasures

While the popular beaches are great, some of my most memorable experiences have been at the hidden, lesser-known spots. These are the places where you can escape the crowds and feel like you've discovered your own private paradise.

Playa de Güigüi

One of the most secluded and beautiful beaches on the island is Playa de Güigüi. Located on the western coast, this beach is a bit of a trek to get to, but it's well worth the effort. You can reach it by hiking from the village of Tasartico, a journey that takes about two hours through rugged terrain. Alternatively, you can take a boat from Puerto de las Nieves.

I opted for the hike, and the experience was incredible. The path winds through dramatic landscapes, and as you descend towards the beach, the view is breathtaking. Once you arrive, you'll find a pristine beach with crystal-clear waters and hardly another soul in sight. It's the perfect spot for a picnic and a swim. Just be sure to bring everything you need, as there are no facilities here.

Playa de Guayedra

Another hidden gem is Playa de Guayedra, near Agaete. This beach is less frequented by tourists, making it a peaceful retreat. The black sand beach is surrounded by towering cliffs, giving it a dramatic and wild feel. I stumbled upon this beach during a road trip around the island, and it quickly became one of my favorites.

The beach is a bit tricky to access, as you'll need to navigate a narrow, winding road, but once you arrive, the seclusion and beauty are worth it. The water here can be a bit rough, so it's best for sunbathing and enjoying the scenery rather than swimming. There's also a small, family-run restaurant nearby, Restaurante El Balcón de Guayedra (Calle Guayedra, 35489 Agaete, +34 928 89 85 20), where you can enjoy a delicious meal with a view.

Playa de Tufia

For a mix of history and natural beauty, check out Playa de Tufia. This small beach is located near the village of Tufia, which is known for its archaeological sites. The beach itself is a charming spot with clear waters, perfect for a quiet day by the sea. What I love most about Tufia is the sense of history that permeates the area. Exploring the ancient caves and ruins gives you a glimpse into the island's past, making it a unique and enriching experience.

The village has a few small restaurants where you can try some local dishes. I recommend El Boya Tufia (Calle Tufia, 13, 35218 Telde, +34 928 68 18 20) for some of the best seafood in the area.

Conclusion

Gran Canaria's beaches are as diverse as they are beautiful, offering something for everyone. Whether you're looking to relax, dive into exciting water activities, or discover hidden coastal treasures, the island's shores are sure to leave you with unforgettable memories. From the lively Playa de Las Canteras to the tranquil Playa de Güigüi, each beach has its own story and charm. As you explore these stunning spots, you'll not only soak up the sun and sea but also a bit of the island's rich culture and natural beauty. Enjoy your time in Gran Canaria, and don't forget to take a moment to simply sit back, relax, and savor the incredible views.

Chapter 5

Experiencing Gran Canaria's Culture

Museums and Galleries

Museo Canario

When I first visited Gran Canaria, I was eager to immerse myself in the local culture and history. The Museo Canario in Las Palmas was my first stop. Nestled in the heart of the Vegueta neighborhood, this museum is a treasure trove of artifacts from the pre-Hispanic era. Walking through its halls, I felt transported back in time, learning about the ancient Guanches, the island's original inhabitants. The exhibits are well-curated, with everything from pottery to mummified remains, providing a fascinating glimpse into the island's past. If you're like me and love diving deep into history, this is a must-visit. The museum is located at Calle del Doctor Verneau, 2, 35001 Las Palmas de Gran Canaria, and their phone number is +34 928 336 800. The entry fee is quite reasonable at €5 for adults and €2.50 for students.

CAAM – Centro Atlántico de Arte Moderno

Art lovers should not miss the CAAM in Las Palmas. This contemporary art museum showcases both local and international artists, offering a vibrant mix of styles and mediums. I was particularly struck by an exhibition of Canarian artists, whose works reflect the unique cultural blend of the islands. The museum itself is a beautiful blend of traditional Canarian architecture and modern design, making the visit enjoyable even before you enter the galleries. Located at Calle los Balcones, 11, 35001 Las Palmas de Gran Canaria, you can reach them at +34 928 311 800. The admission is free, which makes it a fantastic option for those traveling on a budget.

Museo Elder de la Ciencia y la Tecnología

For a more interactive experience, the Museo Elder de la Ciencia y la Tecnología is fantastic, especially if you're traveling with kids. This science and technology museum is packed with hands-on exhibits that are both fun and educational. I spent a delightful afternoon here, exploring everything from robotics to space exploration. The museum is at Parque Santa Catalina, 35007 Las Palmas de Gran Canaria, and the phone number is +34 828 011 828. The entry fee is €6 for adults and €3 for children, making it an affordable family outing.

Festivals and Events

Carnival of Las Palmas

One of my most memorable experiences in Gran Canaria was attending the Carnival of Las Palmas. This vibrant festival, held annually in February, is a whirlwind of color, music, and dance. The entire city comes alive with parades, street parties, and elaborate costumes. I joined the revelers in the streets, dancing to the infectious rhythms of salsa and merengue, and marveling at the creativity and energy of the participants. If you plan your trip around this time, you're in for an unforgettable treat. The main events take place around Parque Santa Catalina, with detailed schedules available closer to the date.

Fiesta de la Rama

Another unique festival is the Fiesta de la Rama in Agaete, held every August. This traditional celebration involves participants carrying branches from the mountains to the sea, mimicking an ancient ritual to bring rain. I participated in the parade, waving a branch and joining in the chants and dances. It was a moving experience, connecting deeply with the island's heritage. The festival culminates in a lively beach party, where everyone, locals and tourists alike, join in the fun.

FISALDO – Feria Internacional de la Artesanía de Las Palmas

For those who appreciate crafts and local artisans, FISALDO is a wonderful event. This international craft fair, held in June, showcases a wide variety of handmade goods, from jewelry to textiles. I bought several unique souvenirs here, each with a story behind it. The fair is held at INFECAR, Avenida de la Feria, 1, 35012 Las Palmas de Gran Canaria, and you can contact them at +34 928 219 797 for more details.

Local Cuisine and Dining

Tapas in Vegueta

No visit to Gran Canaria is complete without indulging in the local cuisine. One of my favorite culinary experiences was a tapas tour in the Vegueta district of Las Palmas. This historic area is dotted with charming bars and restaurants, each offering a variety of small dishes that pack big flavors. I started at La Azotea de Benito, where I savored papas arrugadas (wrinkled potatoes) with mojo sauce, a quintessential Canarian dish. The bar is located at Calle Pelota, 12, 35001 Las Palmas de Gran Canaria, and their phone number is +34 928 332 024. Prices for tapas range from €3 to €6 each, making it easy to sample a variety of dishes.

Casa Montesdeoca

For a more upscale dining experience, I highly recommend Casa Montesdeoca. Housed in a 16th-century building, this restaurant offers a blend of traditional Canarian and modern cuisine. I enjoyed a delectable meal of fresh seafood, paired with local wines. The ambiance is intimate and the service impeccable. You'll find Casa Montesdeoca at Calle Montesdeoca, 10, 35001 Las Palmas de Gran Canaria, and can reach them at +34 928 333 282. Expect to spend around €30-€50 per person.

Mercado del Puerto

If you prefer a more casual setting, head to Mercado del Puerto. This market is a foodie's paradise, with stalls offering everything from fresh seafood to international cuisine. I spent a leisurely afternoon here, sampling grilled octopus, cheese from local dairies, and an array of pastries. The market is at Calle Albareda, 76, 35008 Las Palmas de Gran Canaria, and their phone number is +34 928 469 079. Prices are very reasonable, with most dishes costing between €5 and €15.

El Equilibrista 33

For a unique fusion of Canarian and international flavors, El Equilibrista 33 is a must-visit. I was blown away by their innovative dishes, like the lamb with a gofio (traditional Canarian flour) crust and the exquisite desserts. The restaurant is cozy and stylish, perfect for a romantic dinner. Find it at Calle Pelayo, 15, 35010 Las Palmas de Gran Canaria, and call +34 928 226 872 for reservations. A meal here will cost around €25-€40 per person.

Traditional Music and Dance

Folklore Nights in Teror

One evening, I ventured to the town of Teror, known for its traditional folklore nights. These events are a celebration of Canarian music and dance, held in the picturesque Plaza del Pino. I was captivated by the performances of timple (a small guitar-like instrument) players and folk dancers in vibrant costumes. The atmosphere was electric, with locals and tourists dancing together under the stars. It was one of those magical travel moments that I'll never forget. The best time to catch these performances is during the town's annual fiestas in September.

Noche de Fado in Las Palmas

For something different, I attended a Noche de Fado, a night of traditional Portuguese music, in Las Palmas.

Held at the Casa de Colón, this event features soulful performances by fado singers, accompanied by guitar. The music was deeply moving, and the intimate setting added to the experience. The Casa de Colón is located at Calle Colón, 1, 35001 Las Palmas de Gran Canaria, and you can reach them at +34 928 312 373. The event usually costs around €10-€15.

Romería de San Juan Bautista

During my stay, I was lucky enough to witness the Romería de San Juan Bautista in Telde. This traditional pilgrimage and festival are held in June, featuring processions, music, and dance. Participants dress in traditional Canarian costumes, and the streets are filled with the sounds of folk music and laughter. I joined in the festivities, sampling local delicacies and dancing with the locals. The sense of community and tradition was palpable, making it a truly special experience.

Taberna La Peña

For a more regular dose of traditional music, Taberna La Peña in Las Palmas offers live Canarian music several nights a week. This cozy tavern is a great place to enjoy a meal or a drink while listening to local musicians. I spent a delightful evening here, soaking up the authentic atmosphere and chatting with fellow travelers and locals. The tavern is located at Calle Secretario Artiles, 34, 35007 Las Palmas de Gran Canaria, and their phone number is +34 928 265 795. Meals are reasonably priced, with most dishes under €20.

Exploring Gran Canaria's culture was one of the highlights of my trip. The island's rich history, vibrant festivals, delicious cuisine, and captivating music and dance all come together to create a truly unique and unforgettable experience. Whether you're a history buff, a foodie, or simply looking to soak up the local atmosphere, Gran Canaria has something to offer everyone.

Chapter 6

Outdoor Adventures in Gran Canaria

Gran Canaria is an island that offers more than just stunning beaches and vibrant nightlife. For the outdoor enthusiast, it's a paradise filled with countless adventures waiting to be experienced. From hiking through rugged mountains to exploring lush national parks, engaging in exhilarating water sports, and discovering diverse bird species, Gran Canaria has it all. Let me take you through some of the most memorable outdoor activities that I've enjoyed on this beautiful island.

Hiking and Nature Trails

One of the best ways to explore Gran Canaria's diverse landscape is by hiking. The island boasts an extensive network of trails that cater to all levels of hikers, from easy walks to challenging treks.

Roque Nublo

A must-do hike is the trail to Roque Nublo, one of Gran Canaria's most iconic landmarks. The hike is relatively easy and suitable for families. Starting from the parking area at La Goleta, the trail is about 1.5 kilometers one way and offers breathtaking views of the surrounding landscapes. The pinnacle of the hike is reaching the towering rock formation, Roque Nublo, standing 80 meters tall. The panoramic views from here are simply stunning, especially at sunset.

Address: La Goleta, 35369 Tejeda, Las Palmas

Phone: +34 928 66 33 50

Tip: Wear comfortable hiking shoes and bring plenty of water.

Barranco de Guayadeque

Another fantastic hiking destination is Barranco de Guayadeque. This ravine is not only a natural beauty but also rich in cultural heritage with its cave dwellings. The hike through the ravine is moderately challenging but offers a unique glimpse into the island's history and natural beauty. Don't miss the small chapel and the cave restaurants where you can enjoy a meal inside a cave!

Address: Ingenio, Las Palmas

Phone: +34 928 78 00 76

Tip: Try the local dishes at one of the cave restaurants; the experience is unforgettable.

Tamabada Natural Park

For those looking for a more strenuous hike, Tamabada Natural Park offers some of the most rugged and remote trails on the island. The park is home to diverse flora and fauna and provides a serene escape from the more touristy areas. The trails here can be challenging, so they are best suited for experienced hikers. The effort is rewarded with spectacular views and a deep sense of tranquility.

Address: Artenara, 35350, Las Palmas

Phone: +34 928 88 02 76

Tip: Check the weather forecast before heading out and inform someone about your hiking plans.

National and Natural Parks

Gran Canaria is home to several national and natural parks that are perfect for outdoor adventures and nature lovers.

Caldera de Bandama

Caldera de Bandama is a massive volcanic crater that offers a unique hiking experience. You can hike around the rim of the crater or descend into the caldera itself. The trail around the rim is relatively easy and provides fantastic views of the crater and the surrounding areas. Inside the caldera, you'll find lush vegetation and a vineyard that produces local wines.

Address: Bandama, 35310, Las Palmas

Phone: +34 928 35 00 77

Tip: Visit the nearby Pico de Bandama for even more impressive views.

Dunas de Maspalomas

The Dunas de Maspalomas is a stunning natural reserve that feels like a desert oasis by the sea. The best way to explore the dunes is on foot, but you can also take a camel ride for a unique experience. The dunes are particularly beautiful at sunrise and sunset when the light casts dramatic shadows across the sand.

Address: Maspalomas, 35100, Las Palmas

Phone: +34 928 77 22 00

Tip: Bring a hat and sunscreen; there's little shade in the dunes.

Los Tilos de Moya

Los Tilos de Moya is a beautiful laurel forest that offers a cool, shaded escape from the island's heat. The forest is crisscrossed with walking trails that take you through lush vegetation and alongside babbling streams. It's a perfect spot for a leisurely walk or a picnic.

Address: Moya, 35420, Las Palmas

Phone: +34 928 61 04 00

Tip: Visit the nearby town of Moya for a taste of local culture and cuisine.

Water Activities and Sports

Gran Canaria's coastal location makes it an ideal destination for water sports enthusiasts. Whether you're a seasoned pro or a beginner, there's something for everyone.

Surfing in Playa del Inglés

Playa del Inglés is one of the best spots on the island for surfing. The waves here are suitable for all levels, and there are several surf schools offering lessons and equipment rentals. The beach is also a great place to relax and watch the surfers if you prefer to stay on dry land.

Address: Playa del Inglés, 35100, Las Palmas

Phone: +34 928 77 12 34

Price: Surfboard rental from €15, lessons from €35

Tip: Early morning is the best time to catch the waves.

Snorkeling in Puerto de Mogán

Puerto de Mogán, known as "Little Venice," is a charming town with excellent snorkeling opportunities. The clear, calm waters are home to a variety of marine life, making it a great spot for both beginners and experienced snorkelers. There are several companies offering guided snorkeling tours and equipment rentals.

Address: Puerto de Mogán, 35138, Las Palmas

Phone: +34 928 56 72 00

Price: Snorkeling tours from €25

Tip: Combine your snorkeling trip with a visit to the town's picturesque marina and market.

Sailing and Boat Tours

Exploring Gran Canaria from the water is a must-do experience. There are numerous sailing and boat tours available, ranging from relaxing catamaran cruises to adventurous speedboat rides. Many tours include opportunities for swimming, snorkeling, and dolphin watching.

Address: Various locations around the island

Phone: +34 928 15 00 00

Price: Boat tours from €40

Tip: Book your tour in advance, especially during peak season.

Scuba Diving in Las Palmas

Gran Canaria is a popular destination for scuba diving, thanks to its rich marine life and clear waters. Las Palmas offers several dive sites suitable for all levels, from beginners to advanced divers. There are many dive schools and centers that provide courses, guided dives, and equipment rentals.

Address: Las Palmas, 35001, Las Palmas

Phone: +34 928 46 70 00

Price: Dive courses from €200, single dives from €50

Tip: Make sure to bring your diving certification card if you're planning to dive independently.

Bird Watching

Gran Canaria's diverse habitats make it a fantastic destination for bird watching. Whether you're a seasoned birder or just enjoy observing wildlife, you'll find plenty of opportunities to spot a variety of bird species.

La Charca de Maspalomas

La Charca de Maspalomas is a coastal lagoon located next to the Maspalomas Dunes. It's a haven for birdwatchers, particularly during the migration seasons. Here, you can spot species such as herons, egrets, and various types of waders. The lagoon is easily accessible and provides a peaceful environment for bird watching.

Address: Maspalomas, 35100, Las Palmas

Phone: +34 928 14 00 00

Tip: Bring binoculars and a bird guidebook for the best experience.

Barranco de Azuaje

Barranco de Azuaje is a lush ravine that offers excellent bird-watching opportunities. The area is home to a variety of bird species, including the endemic Gran Canaria blue chaffinch. The ravine's diverse vegetation and water sources attract many birds, making it a great spot for a day of bird watching.

Address: Firgas, 35432, Las Palmas

Phone: +34 928 31 00 00

Tip: Visit early in the morning when bird activity is highest.

Finca de Osorio

Finca de Osorio is a beautiful estate with extensive gardens and forests, providing a habitat for many bird species. It's a perfect spot for a leisurely walk combined with bird watching. The estate is well-maintained and offers a peaceful escape from the more crowded tourist areas.

Address: Teror, 35330, Las Palmas

Phone: +34 928 61 60 00

Tip: Combine your visit with a trip to the nearby town of Teror, known for its charming streets and local markets.

Personal Tips and Final Thoughts

Gran Canaria is a treasure trove of outdoor adventures waiting to be discovered. As someone who has explored its many trails, parks, and coastal waters, I can assure you that there's something for everyone. Whether you're an adrenaline junkie looking for your next thrill or someone who simply enjoys being in nature, Gran Canaria will not disappoint.

Here are a few personal tips to make the most of your outdoor adventures:

1. Plan Ahead: Research the trails and parks you want to visit and check for any access restrictions or weather conditions. It's always a good idea to have a flexible plan.

2. Stay Hydrated: The island's climate can be quite warm, especially during the summer months. Carry plenty of water with you, particularly on longer hikes.

3. Respect Nature: Leave no trace and respect the natural environment. Stick to marked trails and be mindful of wildlife.

4. Engage with Locals: The local people are incredibly friendly and knowledgeable. Don't hesitate to ask for recommendations or directions; it's a great way to discover hidden gems.

5. Enjoy the Moment: Gran Canaria is a place of incredible natural beauty. Take your time, enjoy the views, and make lasting memories.

Exploring Gran Canaria's outdoors has been one of the highlights of my travels. The island's diverse landscapes and abundant activities ensure that every visit is filled with new adventures and unforgettable experiences. Whether it's hiking to a volcanic crater, snorkeling in crystal-clear waters, or spotting rare bird species, Gran Canaria offers endless opportunities for outdoor enthusiasts. I hope this guide inspires you to embark on your own adventure and experience the natural wonders of this incredible island.

Chapter 7

Shopping in Gran Canaria

Local Markets

One of my favorite things about traveling is immersing myself in the local culture, and there's no better place to do that in Gran Canaria than at the local markets. From the bustling stalls to the vibrant colors and tantalizing smells, shopping at these markets is an experience you won't want to miss.

Mercado de Vegueta

My first stop was the Mercado de Vegueta in Las Palmas. Located at Calle Mendizábal, 1, 35001 Las Palmas, this market is a food lover's paradise. As I wandered through the aisles, I was greeted by the friendly faces of vendors selling everything from fresh fruits and vegetables to locally caught fish. The market is open from 6 AM to 2 PM, Monday to Saturday. Don't miss the chance to sample some local delicacies like papas arrugadas (wrinkled potatoes) and gofio, a type of flour made from roasted grains.

I remember chatting with a vendor who insisted I try some local cheeses. I ended up buying a chunk of queso de flor, a deliciously creamy cheese made from sheep's milk. It cost around €8 for a decent-sized piece, and it was worth every penny. If you're looking for a souvenir that truly captures the essence of Gran Canaria, grab some local honey or mojo sauce.

San Mateo Market

Another market that left a lasting impression on me was the San Mateo Market, located in the heart of the mountain town of San Mateo at Calle del Mercado, 1, 35320 Vega de San Mateo. This market is open on weekends from 8 AM to 2:30 PM and offers a more rustic and authentic experience. Here, I found a delightful mix of fresh produce, handmade crafts, and local wines.

One particular vendor sold handmade wooden toys and trinkets that were perfect for bringing back home as gifts. I bought a beautifully carved wooden box for just €15, a keepsake that now holds all my small travel mementos. The friendly locals and the charming atmosphere made my visit to San Mateo Market unforgettable.

Mercado de Puerto

For those staying closer to Las Palmas, the Mercado de Puerto at Calle Albareda, 76, 35008 Las Palmas, is a must-visit. Open daily from 7 AM to 2 PM, this market offers a fantastic array of fresh seafood, meats, and vegetables. I loved the vibrant atmosphere, with locals bustling about and vendors enthusiastically promoting their goods. It's also a great spot to enjoy some tapas and a cold beer.

Shopping Streets

When it comes to shopping streets, Gran Canaria offers a delightful mix of modern shops and charming boutiques. Walking through these streets is a great way to spend an afternoon, even if you're just window shopping.

Calle Triana

One of the most famous shopping streets in Las Palmas is Calle Triana. This pedestrian-friendly street is lined with shops, cafés, and restaurants, making it the perfect place to spend a leisurely day. The street is located in the historic Triana district and stretches from Teatro Pérez Galdós to Parque San Telmo.

As I strolled down Calle Triana, I found everything from high-end fashion stores to quaint local boutiques. One shop that stood out was "El Rincón de Triana," a charming boutique where I bought a beautiful handmade scarf for €25. The quality and craftsmanship were impeccable, and it remains one of my favorite souvenirs from Gran Canaria.

If you get hungry while shopping, there are plenty of places to grab a bite. I highly recommend stopping at "Café Regina" for a coffee and a pastry. Their almond croissants are to die for!

Avenida Mesa y López

Another popular shopping destination is Avenida Mesa y López, which is home to the large department store El Corte Inglés. Located at Av. José Mesa y López, 18, 35006 Las Palmas, this shopping street offers a mix of high-end stores and more affordable options.

El Corte Inglés is a one-stop shop for everything you might need, from fashion and beauty products to electronics and home goods. During my visit, I spent hours browsing the different departments and ended up buying a stylish pair of sunglasses for €30.

Yumbo Centrum

For something a bit different, head to Yumbo Centrum in Playa del Inglés. This shopping center at Av. de España, 35100 Maspalomas, is known for its eclectic mix of shops and lively nightlife. It's open daily from 10 AM to midnight, making it a great place to visit after a day at the beach.

Yumbo Centrum has everything from souvenir shops to designer boutiques. I picked up a few unique souvenirs here, including a hand-painted ceramic tile for €12. The center also has a variety of restaurants and bars, perfect for grabbing a drink and unwinding after a long day of shopping.

Souvenirs and Local Crafts

When it comes to souvenirs, Gran Canaria has a fantastic selection of local crafts that make for perfect keepsakes and gifts. From handmade jewelry to traditional pottery, there's something for everyone.

Artesanía Santa Catalina

One of my favorite places to shop for local crafts is Artesanía Santa Catalina, located at Calle Triana, 46, 35002 Las Palmas. This shop offers a beautiful selection of handmade items, including ceramics, textiles, and jewelry. I bought a stunning pair of silver earrings for €20, made by a local artisan. The intricate design and craftsmanship were truly impressive.

La Molina Artesanía

Another gem is La Molina Artesanía, located in Maspalomas at Av. de Gáldar, 35100 San Bartolomé de Tirajana. This store specializes in traditional Canarian crafts, including pottery, woven baskets, and leather goods. I found a beautifully crafted leather wallet for €35, which has become a cherished item in my collection.

El Mercado de Artesanía de Vegueta

For those interested in a more immersive experience, El Mercado de Artesanía de Vegueta is a must-visit. Held on Sundays at Plaza del Pilar Nuevo, 35001 Las Palmas, this market is a treasure trove of handmade goods. From intricate lacework to colorful ceramics, the market offers a wide range of local crafts.

I remember buying a handwoven basket here for €15. The vendor explained the traditional techniques used to create it, making it even more special. It's now a centerpiece in my living room, filled with memories of my time in Gran Canaria.

Tips for Shopping in Gran Canaria

Bargaining: While bargaining isn't common in most shops, you might try negotiating prices at local markets, especially if you're buying multiple items.

Payment Methods: Most shops and markets accept credit and debit cards, but it's always a good idea to carry some cash, especially for smaller vendors.

Tax-Free Shopping: Non-EU visitors can benefit from tax-free shopping. Make sure to ask for a tax-free form at the time of purchase and keep your receipts. You can claim your refund at the airport before departing.

Opening Hours: Many shops in Gran Canaria follow a siesta schedule, closing in the afternoon and reopening in the evening. Plan your shopping trips accordingly.

Local Produce: Don't miss the chance to buy local produce like fruits, cheeses, and wines. They make for delicious souvenirs and are a great way to bring a taste of Gran Canaria back home.

Shopping in Gran Canaria is more than just a chance to buy souvenirs; it's an opportunity to connect with the local culture and bring a piece of this beautiful island back home with you. Whether you're wandering through bustling markets, exploring charming boutiques, or hunting for unique crafts, the shopping experiences here are bound to be memorable.

Gran Canaria offers a rich tapestry of shopping experiences that cater to all tastes and budgets. From the vibrant local markets to the bustling shopping streets and unique local crafts, there is something for everyone. Embrace the adventure, take your time to explore, and don't forget to engage with the friendly locals who make this island such a special place to visit. Happy shopping!

Chapter 8

Nightlife and Entertainment in Gran Canaria

Gran Canaria has a way of coming alive as the sun sets, transforming from a sunny paradise into a vibrant hub of nightlife and entertainment. As someone who has experienced this island both under the golden sun and beneath the sparkling stars, I can tell you that the nightlife here is something you don't want to miss. Whether you're looking for a quiet evening with a good drink, a night of dancing until dawn, or a cultural outing, Gran Canaria has it all. Let me take you through some of my favorite spots.

Bars and Pubs

Gran Canaria's bar scene is diverse, offering everything from cozy, traditional pubs to chic, modern lounges. One of my favorite spots is The Paper Club in Las Palmas. Located at Calle Remedios, 10, 35002 Las Palmas de Gran Canaria, this bar offers a laid-back atmosphere with live music and a great selection of cocktails. The last time I was there, I enjoyed a refreshing mojito while listening to an incredible local band. The drinks are reasonably priced, with cocktails around €7-€9. You can call them at +34 928 38 14 23 for more information.

Another gem is El Gallinero Café Arte. This artistic bar is located at Calle Cano, 7, 35002 Las Palmas de Gran Canaria. It's a cozy, bohemian spot perfect for unwinding with friends. They often host art exhibitions and live music performances. A glass of wine here costs about €4, and their tapas are delightful. Contact them at +34 606 63 40 67 to check their event schedule.

For a more traditional pub experience, The Shamrock Bar in Playa del Inglés is your go-to spot. Situated at Avenida de España, C.C. Yumbo, 35100 Maspalomas, this Irish pub offers live sports, great beers, and a lively atmosphere. I remember enjoying a hearty pint of Guinness while cheering for my favorite football team. Prices for drinks range from €3-€6. Give them a ring at +34 928 76 71 00.

Nightclubs

If dancing the night away is more your style, Gran Canaria's nightclub scene won't disappoint. Pacha Gran Canaria in Playa del Inglés is one of the most famous clubs on the island. Located at Avenida Sargentos Provisionales, 10, 35100 Maspalomas, it offers an energetic atmosphere with top DJs and a spacious dance floor. I had an unforgettable night here, losing myself in the music and the vibrant crowd. Entry fees vary but expect to pay around €10-€20, with drinks costing about €8 each. For reservations, call +34 928 76 76 30.

Another fantastic spot is Chester Club & Lounge. This upscale club at Avenida de Italia, 13, 35100 Playa del Inglés offers a more refined experience. The stylish décor, combined with excellent music and service, makes it a great place to spend a sophisticated night out. The entrance fee is usually around €15, and cocktails are priced at €10-€12. You can contact them at +34 696 78 92 07 for more details.

For a more unique experience, check out Club Bukaro. Nestled in Puerto Rico at Avenida de la Cornisa, 21, 35130 Mogán, this club offers stunning views and an eclectic mix of music. I enjoyed a night here dancing under the stars with a beautiful view of the marina. Entry fees are about €10, and drinks range from €7-€10. Their phone number is +34 928 72 82 56.

Live Music Venues

If live music is your passion, Gran Canaria has plenty to offer. La Guarida del Blues in Las Palmas is a must-visit. Located at Calle Mendizábal, 17, 35001 Las Palmas de Gran Canaria, this venue specializes in blues and jazz. I had an amazing evening here, sipping on a cold beer and getting lost in the soulful tunes. Entrance is usually free, but it's good to call ahead at +34 928 38 18 07 to check the lineup.

For a more eclectic music scene, The Paper Club also serves as a live music venue with a diverse range of performances. As mentioned earlier, it's a great place to discover local talent and enjoy a variety of music genres.

Another favorite of mine is Plaza de la Música in Las Palmas. This open-air venue at Avenida de la Feria, 1, 35012 Las Palmas de Gran Canaria hosts a variety of concerts and festivals. I remember attending a fantastic rock concert here, with the sea breeze adding to the electrifying atmosphere. Check their schedule online or call +34 928 41 58 67 for upcoming events.

Theatres and Cinemas

For those who prefer a quieter evening, Gran Canaria's theatres and cinemas offer plenty of entertainment options. Teatro Pérez Galdós in Las Palmas is an architectural gem and a cultural hotspot. Located at Plaza Stagno, 1, 35002 Las Palmas de Gran Canaria, this historic theatre hosts a range of performances from opera to contemporary plays. I had the pleasure of attending an opera here, and the experience was nothing short of magical. Tickets vary depending on the show, but expect to pay around €20-€50. Their contact number is +34 928 36 06 00.

For movie lovers, Multicines Monopol offers a great cinematic experience. Situated at Plaza Hurtado de Mendoza, 1, 35002 Las Palmas de Gran Canaria, this cinema showcases both mainstream and indie films. I enjoyed watching a Spanish indie film here, and the intimate setting made it all the more special. Ticket prices are around €7-€9. You can call them at +34 928 37 80 52 for showtimes.

Another great option is Yelmo Cines Alisios. Located at C.C. Alisios, Carretera Tamaraceite, 35119 Las Palmas de Gran Canaria, this modern cinema offers the latest releases in a comfortable setting. I loved the plush seating and high-quality sound system. Tickets cost between €8-€10. Their phone number is +34 928 47 44 43.

Using Google Maps to Find Locations

When you're in Gran Canaria, getting to these fantastic nightlife spots is easy with Google Maps. Here's a simple guide on how to use it:

Open Google Maps: On your smartphone, open the Google Maps app.

Search for the Destination: Type the name or address of the place you want to visit in the search bar.

Get Directions: Click on the location's name that appears on the map. Tap the "Directions" button.

Choose Your Mode of Transport: Select whether you're walking, driving, or using public transportation.

Follow the Route: Google Maps will show you the best route from your current location. Follow the directions given.

For example, if you want to visit The Paper Club, you would:

Open Google Maps and type "The Paper Club, Calle Remedios, 10, 35002 Las Palmas de Gran Canaria".

Tap on the location and then tap "Directions".

Choose your mode of transport and follow the route.

This way, you can easily explore Gran Canaria's vibrant nightlife without worrying about getting lost.

Gran Canaria's nightlife and entertainment options are as diverse and exciting as the island itself. From sipping cocktails at a cozy bar to dancing the night away at a bustling nightclub, or enjoying a live music performance to watching a play in a historic theatre, there's something for everyone. As someone who has experienced the island's nightlife first-hand, I can promise you that your evenings here will be just as memorable as your days. So, grab your dancing shoes, put on your best outfit, and get ready to explore Gran Canaria's vibrant after-dark scene. Cheers to unforgettable nights!

Chapter 9

What to Do and Not to Do in Gran Canaria

Gran Canaria is a treasure trove of stunning landscapes, rich culture, and warm, welcoming people. I've had the pleasure of exploring its many facets, and I want to share some insights to help you make the most of your visit. Here's a comprehensive guide on what to do and not to do in Gran Canaria, ensuring you respect local customs, stay safe, avoid common mistakes, and engage in responsible tourism.

Respecting Local Customs and Traditions

Gran Canaria, like the rest of Spain, is a place where traditions run deep. Embracing these customs will not only enrich your experience but also show respect to the locals.

Greeting Etiquette:

When meeting someone, a polite "Hola" (hello) or "Buenos días" (good morning) goes a long way. For more formal interactions, you might say "Buenas tardes" (good afternoon) or "Buenas noches" (good evening). In social settings, it's common to greet with a kiss on each cheek, starting with the right. However, if you're not sure, a friendly handshake will do.

Dress Code:

While Gran Canaria is laid-back, it's good to dress appropriately, especially when visiting religious sites like the Catedral de Santa Ana in Las Palmas. Avoid wearing beachwear in the city or in restaurants. Pack light, breathable clothes for the day and something slightly dressier for evenings out.

Dining Etiquette:

Meal times in Spain are different. Lunch is usually between 2 PM and 4 PM, and dinner rarely starts before 9 PM. If you're invited to a local's home, it's polite to bring a small gift, like wine or sweets. When dining out, tipping is appreciated but not mandatory; leaving about 5-10% is a nice gesture.

Festivals and Celebrations:

Participate in local festivals like Carnival or the Fiesta de San Juan. These are fantastic opportunities to immerse yourself in the culture. Just remember to be respectful of the customs and traditions being celebrated.

Safety Tips

Gran Canaria is generally a safe destination, but like anywhere, it's wise to stay aware and take precautions.

Personal Safety:

The island is quite safe, but petty theft can occur, especially in crowded areas like markets or festivals. Keep an eye on your belongings, use a money belt, and avoid displaying valuables.

Emergency Contacts:

In case of emergencies, dial 112 for police, fire, or medical services. It's handy to have the contact information of your country's embassy as well.

Beach Safety:

Gran Canaria boasts beautiful beaches, but it's important to swim in designated areas and heed warning flags. Red flags indicate dangerous conditions, while yellow means caution. Lifeguards are usually present, but always be cautious.

Health Precautions:

Carry a small first-aid kit with essentials like band-aids, antiseptic wipes, and any personal medications. The sun can be strong, so use sunscreen with high SPF, wear hats, and stay hydrated. Tap water is safe to drink, but bottled water is readily available if you prefer.

Local Laws:

Smoking is prohibited in indoor public places and certain outdoor areas like playgrounds. Drug use is illegal, and penalties are severe. Also, public drunkenness is frowned upon and can lead to fines.

Common Tourist Mistakes

Even seasoned travelers can slip up. Here are some common mistakes to avoid:

Overpacking:

Gran Canaria's weather is mild year-round. Light, comfortable clothing is key. Overpacking not only makes travel cumbersome but can also incur extra baggage fees. A versatile wardrobe with layers for cooler evenings will suffice.

Ignoring Siesta Time:

Many shops and businesses close for a siesta between 1 PM and 4 PM. Plan your shopping and activities accordingly to avoid disappointment.

Not Reserving Restaurants:

Popular restaurants can get busy, especially during peak tourist season. Make reservations to ensure you get a table at your desired dining spot.

Underestimating the Sun:

The sun in Gran Canaria can be quite intense. I made the mistake of skipping sunscreen once and paid the price with a nasty sunburn. Apply and reapply sunscreen, wear a hat, and seek shade during peak hours.

Skipping Local Experiences:

Tourist hotspots are great, but don't miss out on local experiences. Visit local markets, dine at small eateries, and engage with locals. These experiences often turn out to be the most memorable.

Responsible Tourism

Traveling responsibly means making choices that benefit the local community and environment. Here's how you can be a responsible tourist in Gran Canaria:

Support Local Businesses:

Instead of international chains, opt for local hotels, restaurants, and shops. This supports the local economy and offers a more authentic experience.

Eco-Friendly Practices:

Gran Canaria's natural beauty is one of its main attractions. Help preserve it by reducing waste, recycling, and avoiding single-use plastics. Bring a reusable water bottle and shopping bag.

Wildlife Respect:

When exploring natural areas, maintain a respectful distance from wildlife and avoid feeding animals. Stick to marked trails to protect the environment.

Cultural Sensitivity:

Respect local customs and traditions. Learn a few basic Spanish phrases; even a simple "Gracias" (thank you) is appreciated. Be mindful of local norms and dress codes, especially in religious or rural areas.

Water Conservation:

Gran Canaria can experience water shortages. Conserve water by taking shorter showers, reusing towels, and turning off the tap while brushing your teeth.

Using Google Maps to Fetch Location Addresses

One of the best tools for navigating Gran Canaria is Google Maps. Here's how to make the most of it:

Finding an Address:

Open Google Maps on your phone. In the search bar, type the name of the place you're looking for. For example, if you want to visit Las Canteras Beach, type "Las Canteras Beach."

Getting Directions:

Once you've found your location, tap on it to bring up more details. Then, select the "Directions" button. Google Maps will use your current location to provide step-by-step directions, whether you're walking, driving, or taking public transportation.

Saving Locations:

If you find a place you want to visit later, tap on "Save" and choose a list to save it to, like "Favorites" or "Want to Go." This makes it easy to plan your itinerary.

Offline Maps:

To save on data, download offline maps. Go to the menu, select "Offline maps," then "Select your own map." Zoom in on the area you'll be visiting and hit "Download."

Exploring Nearby:

Use the "Explore" feature to find nearby attractions, restaurants, and more. Tap on the search bar, then select "Explore nearby." You'll get a list of places categorized by type.

By following these tips, you can navigate Gran Canaria like a pro, ensuring you find all the best spots and make the most of your visit.

Personal Experiences

One of my favorite experiences in Gran Canaria was visiting the Maspalomas Dunes. Walking through the golden sands felt like stepping into a different world. I recommend going early in the morning to catch the sunrise; the play of light over the dunes is simply magical.

For a taste of local culture, I visited the Mercado de Vegueta in Las Palmas. The vibrant market is a feast for the senses, with stalls brimming with fresh produce, cheeses, and local delicacies. I chatted with friendly vendors, sampled delicious chorizo, and picked up some unique souvenirs.

Dining at a small, family-run restaurant in Agaete was another highlight. The owner, Maria, treated me like family, and the food was incredible. Her homemade papas arrugadas (wrinkled potatoes) with mojo sauce were the best I've ever had. If you're in Agaete, look for Restaurante Casa Maria at Calle Juan de Bethencourt Domínguez, 24, 35480 Agaete. You won't be disappointed.

In conclusion, Gran Canaria is a place of endless beauty and charm. By respecting local customs, staying safe, avoiding common mistakes, and practicing responsible tourism, you'll have a fulfilling and enjoyable stay. And remember, the best experiences often come from stepping off the beaten path and immersing yourself in the local way of life. Enjoy your adventure!

Chapter 10

Itineraries and Sample Plans

Weekend Getaway

Spending a weekend in Gran Canaria is like diving headfirst into a pool of rich culture, stunning landscapes, and endless fun. Whether you're a seasoned traveler or it's your first visit, there's something about this island that captivates and enchants. Let me walk you through an ideal weekend getaway.

Day 1: Arrival and Beach Bliss

Morning:

Check-in: Start your day by checking into your accommodation. If you're looking for luxury, I recommend Hotel Riu Palace Meloneras (address: Urbanización Las Meloneras, s/n, 35100 Maspalomas,

Gran Canaria, Spain; phone: +34 928 14 02 12). For a more budget-friendly option, consider Bungalows Cordial Green Golf (address: Av. Touroperador Air Marín, s/n, 35100 Maspalomas, Gran Canaria, Spain; phone: +34 928 77 11 66).

Afternoon:

Las Canteras Beach: Head straight to Las Canteras Beach. This urban beach is perfect for a relaxing swim or a sunbathing session. There's nothing like feeling the golden sand beneath your feet. For lunch, grab a bite at La Marinera (address: Paseo las Canteras, 1, 35008 Las Palmas de Gran Canaria, Spain; phone: +34 928 46 31 63). Their seafood paella is a must-try and costs around €15.

Evening:

Sunset at Maspalomas Dunes: In the evening, make your way to the Maspalomas Dunes. Watching the sunset here is a surreal experience. The dunes stretch out like a miniature desert, creating a perfect backdrop for your Instagram photos.

Day 2: Exploring the Heart of Gran Canaria

Morning:

Vegueta: Begin your day exploring Vegueta, the old town of Las Palmas. Wander through its narrow streets, visit the Casa de Colón (address: Calle Colón, 1, 35001 Las Palmas de Gran Canaria, Spain; phone: +34 928 31 23 73), and soak in the historical charm. Entry is free, but donations are welcome.

Afternoon:

Tapas Lunch: Enjoy a tapas lunch at La Vegueta (address: Calle Mendizábal, 3, 35001 Las Palmas de Gran Canaria, Spain; phone: +34 928 33 45 15). Try their papas arrugadas with mojo sauce for around €7.

Evening:

Roque Nublo: In the late afternoon, drive to Roque Nublo. It's one of the island's most iconic natural landmarks. The hike to the top takes about 30-45 minutes, and the views are breathtaking. Make sure to wear comfortable shoes!

Day 3: Farewell and Final Explorations

Morning:

Agaete and Puerto de las Nieves: If you have a bit of time before your flight, visit the charming town of Agaete and its port, Puerto de las Nieves. Stroll along the coast and enjoy the laid-back vibe.

Afternoon:

Lunch and Departure: Have a final meal at Dedo de Dios (address: Calle Nuestra Señora de Las Nieves, s/n, 35480 Agaete, Las Palmas, Spain; phone: +34 928 88 19 57). Their grilled fish is a delight and costs around €18. After lunch, head to the airport for your departure.

Cultural Immersion

For those wanting to dive deep into the local culture, Gran Canaria offers a wealth of experiences that will make you feel like a local in no time.

Day 1: Historical and Artistic Exploration

Morning:

Museo Canario: Start your cultural journey at Museo Canario (address: Calle del Dr. Verneau, 2, 35001 Las Palmas de Gran Canaria, Spain; phone: +34 928 33 65 76). This museum provides a fascinating insight into the island's indigenous Guanche culture. Entry fee is €5.

Afternoon:

Lunch at El Herreño: Enjoy a traditional Canarian lunch at El Herreño (address: Calle Mendizábal, 27, 35001 Las Palmas de Gran Canaria, Spain; phone: +34 928 33 59 89). Try the sancocho canario for around €10.

Evening:

CAAM (Centro Atlántico de Arte Moderno): Spend your evening at CAAM (address: Calle Los Balcones,

11, 35001 Las Palmas de Gran Canaria, Spain; phone: +34 928 31 18 00), where you can explore contemporary art exhibitions. Entry is €3.

Day 2: Festivals and Local Traditions

Morning:

Vegueta Market: Visit the Vegueta Market (address: Calle Mendizábal, 7, 35001 Las Palmas de Gran Canaria, Spain; phone: +34 928 33 22 29) to experience the hustle and bustle of local life. Sample fresh produce and Canarian delicacies.

Afternoon:

Festivals: Depending on the time of year, you might catch one of the island's vibrant festivals. The Fiesta de San Juan in June is a highlight, with bonfires and beach parties.

Evening:

Traditional Music and Dance: Head to a local bar like La Trastienda (address: Calle Pelota, 12, 35001 Las

Palmas de Gran Canaria, Spain; phone: +34 928 33 45 09) for live folk music. The Canarian timple is a unique instrument worth listening to.

Day 3: Gastronomic Delights

Morning:

Cooking Class: Take a cooking class to learn how to make traditional dishes. Taste Gran Canaria (phone: +34 928 33 22 23) offers classes where you can learn to cook mojo sauce and gofio.

Afternoon:

Wine Tasting: Visit a local winery like Bodega Los Berrazales (address: Valle de Agaete, s/n, 35489 San Pedro, Las Palmas, Spain; phone: +34 928 88 15 19). A tasting session costs around €10.

Evening:

Dinner at La Aquarela: For a gourmet experience, dine at La Aquarela (address: Barranco de la Verga, s/n, 35120 Arguineguín, Gran Canaria, Spain; phone: +34

928 73 04 82). Their tasting menu is €90 and showcases the best of Canarian cuisine.

Outdoor Adventure

If you're an adrenaline junkie or simply love the outdoors, Gran Canaria has endless options for you. From hiking and cycling to water sports, this island is an adventurer's paradise.

Day 1: Hiking and Cycling

Morning:

Hiking in Tamadaba Natural Park: Start your adventure with a hike in Tamadaba Natural Park. The trails here are well-marked, and the views are spectacular. Don't forget your camera!

Afternoon:

Lunch at Restaurante El Balcón de Zamora: Enjoy a hearty lunch at Restaurante El Balcón de Zamora (address: Calle Drago, 2, 35457 Artenara, Gran Canaria,

Spain; phone: +34 928 66 77 75). Their goat stew is a local favorite and costs €12.

Evening:

Cycling in Ayagaures: Rent a bike from Free Motion (address: Av. de Italia, 4, 35100 Playa del Inglés, Gran Canaria, Spain; phone: +34 928 77 12 19) and cycle through the scenic Ayagaures valley. Rentals start at €15 per day.

Day 2: Water Sports and More

Morning:

Surfing at Playa del Inglés: Take a surfing lesson at Surf Canaries (address: Av. de Italia, 15, 35100 Playa del Inglés, Gran Canaria, Spain; phone: +34 928 77 11 33). A 2-hour lesson costs €35.

Afternoon:

Lunch at Restaurante La Roca: Refuel at Restaurante La Roca (address: Calle Mar Mediterráneo, 6, 35100 San Bartolomé de Tirajana, Gran Canaria, Spain;

phone: +34 928 72 25 13). Try their fresh fish platter for around €18.

Evening:

Snorkeling at Amadores Beach: End your day with a snorkeling session at Amadores Beach. The clear waters make it perfect for spotting marine life. Rent gear from Dive Academy Gran Canaria (address: Calle San Cristóbal de la Laguna, 7, 35130 Mogán, Gran Canaria, Spain; phone: +34 928 56 11 23) for €20.

Day 3: More Adventures

Morning:

Paragliding: Experience the thrill of paragliding with Sky Rebels (address: Av. de Gran Canaria, 24, 35130 Mogán, Gran Canaria, Spain; phone: +34 618 07 70 83). A tandem flight costs €90.

Afternoon:

Lunch at La Cabaña: Have lunch at La Cabaña (address: Calle Hoya de la Prensa, 1, 35018 Las Palmas de Gran

Canaria, Spain; phone: +34 928 31 16 09). Their Canarian potatoes are a must-try, costing around €6.

Evening:

Stargazing in Tejeda: Head to Tejeda, one of the best spots on the island for stargazing. The clear skies provide a mesmerizing view of the stars. Bring a blanket and some snacks, and enjoy a peaceful night under the cosmos.

Family-Friendly Trip

Gran Canaria is a fantastic destination for families, offering activities and attractions that cater to all ages. Here's a guide to a family-friendly trip.

Day 1: Fun and Relaxation

Morning:

Visit Palmitos Park: Start your day with a visit to Palmitos Park (address: Barranco de Los Palmitos, s/n, 35109 Maspalomas, Gran Canaria, Spain; phone: +34

928 79 70 70). This botanical garden and zoo is perfect for kids. Tickets are €30 for adults and €22 for children.

Afternoon:

Lunch at Restaurante A. Gaudí: Have lunch at Restaurante A. Gaudí (address: Av. de Gran Canaria, 24, 35100 Playa del Inglés, Gran Canaria, Spain; phone: +34 928 77 60 16). Their kid-friendly menu includes delicious pizzas starting at €8.

Evening:

Beach Time at Anfi del Mar: Spend the evening at Anfi del Mar, a family-friendly beach with calm waters perfect for swimming. There are plenty of activities like pedal boats and a playground for kids.

Day 2: Theme Park Adventures

Morning:

Holiday World Maspalomas: Spend your morning at Holiday World Maspalomas (address: Av. Touroperador Tui, 35100 Maspalomas, Gran Canaria,

Spain; phone: +34 928 73 04 09). This amusement park has rides and attractions for all ages. Entry fee is €15.

Afternoon:

Lunch at Mundo: Enjoy lunch at Mundo (address: Av. de Touroperador Tui, s/n, 35100 Maspalomas, Gran Canaria, Spain; phone: +34 928 73 04 56). Their family platter costs €25 and is enough for four.

Evening:

Explore the Yumbo Centrum: Visit the Yumbo Centrum (address: Av. de España, 35100 Playa del Inglés, Gran Canaria, Spain; phone: +34 928 76 01 00) for shopping and entertainment. There are plenty of kid-friendly shops and entertainment options.

Day 3: Nature and Wildlife

Morning:

Visit to Cocodrilo Park: Start your day with a visit to Cocodrilo Park (address: Ctra. General Los Corralillos,

Km 5.5, 35118 Agüimes, Gran Canaria, Spain; phone: +34 928 78 45 25). This rescue center is home to crocodiles, monkeys, and other animals. Tickets are €10 for adults and €6 for children.

Afternoon:

Lunch at Restaurante Mirador La Noria: Enjoy lunch at Restaurante Mirador La Noria (address: Calle Pérez Galdós, 2, 35118 Agüimes, Gran Canaria, Spain; phone: +34 928 78 45 80). Their grilled meats are a hit with families and cost around €15.

Evening:

Explore the Butterfly House: End your day with a visit to the Butterfly House (address: Calle Drago, 7, 35457 Artenara, Gran Canaria, Spain; phone: +34 928 66 78 99). It's a magical experience for kids and adults alike.

Budget Travel

Traveling on a budget doesn't mean missing out on the fun. Gran Canaria offers plenty of affordable

experiences that will leave you with unforgettable
memories.

Day 1: Affordable Exploration

Morning:

Free Walking Tour: Start your day with a free walking
tour of Las Palmas. These tours usually meet at
Parque San Telmo and give you a great overview of
the city. Don't forget to tip your guide!

Afternoon:

Lunch at Mercado del Puerto: Have an affordable
lunch at Mercado del Puerto (address: Calle Albareda,
76, 35008 Las Palmas de Gran Canaria, Spain; phone:
+34 928 46 32 14). You can find various local dishes
for under €10.

Evening:

Stroll Along Las Canteras Beach: Spend your evening strolling along Las Canteras Beach. It's free to enjoy and the perfect spot to watch the sunset.

Day 2: Nature and Adventure

Morning:

Hike in Bandama Caldera: Head to Bandama Caldera for a budget-friendly hike. The views are stunning and it's a great way to explore the natural beauty of the island.

Afternoon:

Lunch at a Local Tapa Bar: Enjoy a budget-friendly lunch at La Tasca de Enfrente (address: Calle Mendizábal, 27, 35001 Las Palmas de Gran Canaria, Spain; phone: +34 928 33 59 89). Tapas here cost around €3 each.

Evening:

Visit the Botanical Garden: Visit the Jardín Botánico Canario Viera y Clavijo (address: Carretera del Centro,

Km 7, 35017 Las Palmas de Gran Canaria, Spain; phone: +34 928 21 95 80). Entry is free and it's a lovely place to relax.

Day 3: Cultural Experiences

Morning:

Visit to the Elder Museum of Science and Technology: Start your day at the Elder Museum of Science and Technology (address: Parque Santa Catalina, s/n, 35007 Las Palmas de Gran Canaria, Spain; phone: +34 928 01 35 30). Entry fee is €6.

Afternoon:

Lunch at a Local Café: Have lunch at Café Domo (address: Calle Triana, 20, 35002 Las Palmas de Gran Canaria, Spain; phone: +34 928 33 22 18). A sandwich and drink combo costs around €5.

Evening:

Explore Vegueta: Spend your evening exploring the old town of Vegueta. The architecture is beautiful and it's free to wander around and take in the sights.

How to Use Google Maps to Fetch Location Address

If you're unfamiliar with using Google Maps to fetch locations, here's a simple guide to help you find the addresses listed from your current location:

Open Google Maps: On your smartphone, tablet, or computer, open the Google Maps app or go to maps.google.com.

Search for the Location: In the search bar at the top, type in the name of the location you want to visit (e.g., "Hotel Riu Palace Meloneras").

Get Directions: Click on the location in the search results. Once the location's information pops up, click on the "Directions" button.

Enter Your Current Location: In the directions panel, enter your current location or use the "Your location" option.

Choose Your Mode of Transport: Select your preferred mode of transport (e.g., car, walking, public transport).

Follow the Directions: Google Maps will provide step-by-step directions to your destination. Follow these directions to reach your location.

By using Google Maps, you can easily navigate your way around Gran Canaria and make the most of your trip. Whether you're hiking up Roque Nublo or finding a hidden beach, Google Maps will be your trusty guide.

Chapter 11

Accommodation in Gran Canaria

When it comes to finding a place to stay in Gran Canaria, the options are as diverse as the island itself. Having spent quite a bit of time exploring this beautiful destination, I can tell you firsthand that there's something for every type of traveler. Whether you're looking for luxury, budget-friendly spots, charming boutique guesthouses, or unique stays that offer something different, Gran Canaria has got you covered. Let me share some of my personal experiences and tips to help you find the perfect accommodation for your trip.

Overview of Accommodation Options

Gran Canaria is a destination that truly caters to all kinds of travelers. From the bustling tourist areas in the south to the tranquil, more traditional settings in the north, the island offers a wide range of accommodations. The key is to choose a place that aligns with your travel goals and preferences.

For those seeking luxury, the island's high-end resorts provide top-notch amenities, stunning views, and exceptional service. If you're traveling on a budget, there are plenty of affordable hotels that offer great value without compromising comfort. For a more intimate and personalized experience, boutique guesthouses are an excellent choice. And for those who want something a bit different, Gran Canaria boasts a variety of unique stays, from eco-friendly lodges to historic buildings.

Luxury Resorts

Staying at a luxury resort in Gran Canaria is like stepping into a paradise within paradise. One of my favorite spots is the Seaside Grand Hotel Residencia in Maspalomas. Nestled among lush gardens and with views of the Maspalomas Dunes, this place is the epitome of luxury. The rooms are spacious and beautifully decorated, and the service is impeccable. A night's stay here can set you back around €400, but it's worth every penny.

Seaside Grand Hotel Residencia

Address: Avenida del Oasis, 32, 35100 Maspalomas, Las Palmas, Spain

Phone: +34 928 723100

Another standout is the Lopesan Baobab Resort, also in Maspalomas. This African-themed resort is perfect for families and couples alike. The resort features several pools, fantastic dining options, and activities for all ages. Prices start at around €250 per night.

Lopesan Baobab Resort

Address: Mar Adriático, 1, 35100 Meloneras, Las Palmas, Spain

Phone: +34 928 154400

Budget-Friendly Hotels

Not everyone travels with a big budget, and that's perfectly okay because Gran Canaria has plenty of affordable yet comfortable hotels. One of the best experiences I had was at the Hotel Parque in Las Palmas. It's centrally located, making it easy to explore the city. The rooms are clean and cozy, and the staff is incredibly friendly. Prices here start at about €60 per night.

Hotel Parque

Address: Muelle Las Palmas, 2, 35003 Las Palmas de Gran Canaria, Las Palmas, Spain

Phone: +34 928 368000

For those looking to stay near the beach, the Hotel Verol in Las Palmas is a great choice. Just a short walk from Las Canteras Beach, this hotel offers comfortable rooms at a very reasonable price, starting around €50 per night.

Hotel Verol

Address: Sagasta, 25, 35008 Las Palmas de Gran Canaria, Las Palmas, Spain

Phone: +34 928 274142

Boutique Guesthouses

If you're after a more intimate and unique experience, boutique guesthouses are the way to go. I once stayed at the charming Casa Mozart in Las Palmas, and it was a delightful experience. This small guesthouse has just a few rooms, each uniquely decorated with a lot of attention to detail. The personal touch from the hosts makes all the difference. Rooms start at about €90 per night.

Casa Mozart

Address: C. Mozart, 2, 35005 Las Palmas de Gran Canaria, Las Palmas, Spain

Phone: +34 630 006623

In the village of Agüimes, there's a wonderful guesthouse called Casa de los Camellos. It's housed in a historic building and offers a very authentic Canarian experience. Staying here feels like a step back in time, with modern comforts. Prices are around €70 per night.

Casa de los Camellos

Address: C. Progreso, 12, 35260 Agüimes, Las Palmas, Spain

Phone: +34 928 785019

Unique Stays

For travelers looking for something out of the ordinary, Gran Canaria offers a variety of unique stays. One of my favorites is the EcoTara Canary Islands Eco-Village Retreat. Located in the heart of the island, this eco-friendly retreat offers yurts and eco-lodges amidst nature. It's perfect for those who want to disconnect and enjoy some peace and quiet. Prices start at around €100 per night.

EcoTara Canary Islands Eco-Village Retreat

Address: Las Rosas 16, 35329 Telde, Las Palmas, Spain

Phone: +34 633 728968

Another unique option is the Parador de Cruz de Tejeda. This hotel is set in a historic building high in the mountains, offering stunning views of the island. It's a great place for hikers and nature lovers. Rooms start at around €120 per night.

Parador de Cruz de Tejeda

Address: Cruz de Tejeda, s/n, 35328 Tejeda, Las Palmas, Spain

Phone: +34 928 012500

Using Google Maps to Fetch Location Addresses

When you're navigating a new place, Google Maps is an indispensable tool. Here's a stylish way to use it to fetch the addresses listed from your current location.

Open Google Maps: On your smartphone, open the Google Maps app. Make sure your location services are turned on.

Search for the Location: Enter the name of the place you want to find in the search bar. For example, type "Seaside Grand Hotel Residencia" if you're looking for that luxury resort.

Get Directions: Once the location appears, tap on it. You'll see a button that says "Directions." Tap on it to see the route from your current location.

Choose Your Mode of Transport: Google Maps will give you options for driving, walking, biking, or public transport. Choose the one that suits you best.

Start Navigation: Tap "Start" to begin navigation. Google Maps will guide you turn-by-turn until you reach your destination.

Save the Address: If you frequently visit a place, you can save it by tapping "Save" and adding it to your favorites or a custom list.

Using Google Maps makes getting around Gran Canaria a breeze, and it ensures you can always find your way to the amazing accommodations and attractions on the island.

In conclusion, Gran Canaria offers a plethora of accommodation options to suit every traveler's needs. Whether you're looking for luxurious pampering, budget-friendly comfort, charming boutique stays, or unique experiences, you're sure to find the perfect place to rest your head. And with tools like Google Maps, navigating to these wonderful spots is easier than ever. So, pack your bags and get ready to explore the diverse and beautiful island of Gran Canaria!

Chapter 12

Top Recommended Hotels and Resorts

Welcome to one of my favorite parts of planning a trip: choosing where to stay! Gran Canaria offers an incredible variety of accommodation options, from luxurious resorts to budget-friendly hotels, family-friendly havens, and cozy spots perfect for couples. I've had the pleasure of experiencing a range of these places, and I'm excited to share my top recommendations with you. Let's dive in!

Best for Luxury

When it comes to luxury, Gran Canaria doesn't disappoint. The island is home to some truly stunning resorts that offer everything you could dream of for a pampered getaway.

1. Seaside Grand Hotel Residencia

Address: Avenida del Oasis, 32, 35100 Maspalomas, Las Palmas

Phone: +34 928 72 30 00

Price Range: €400 - €600 per night

The Seaside Grand Hotel Residencia is the epitome of luxury. Nestled in the heart of Maspalomas, this five-star resort offers breathtaking views, impeccable service, and a serene atmosphere. From the moment I walked into the beautifully designed lobby, I knew I was in for a treat. The rooms are spacious, elegantly decorated, and come with private balconies or terraces. The pool area is a perfect spot to unwind, and the on-site spa offers a range of treatments that left me feeling rejuvenated.

2. Hotel Riu Palace Meloneras

Address: Urbanización Las Meloneras, 35100 Maspalomas, Las Palmas

Phone: +34 928 14 20 77

Price Range: €300 - €450 per night

Staying at the Hotel Riu Palace Meloneras was like a dream. The resort combines modern amenities with traditional Canarian architecture. My room had a stunning view of the ocean, and I spent countless hours relaxing by the infinity pool that seems to blend into the sea. The buffet breakfast was a highlight, offering a wide variety of fresh and delicious options. This place is perfect if you're looking to indulge in a bit of luxury without feeling overwhelmed.

Best for Budget

Traveling on a budget doesn't mean you have to compromise on comfort or experience. Gran Canaria has plenty of great options that offer excellent value for money.

1. Hotel Aloe Canteras

Address: Calle Sagasta, 98, 35008 Las Palmas de Gran Canaria, Las Palmas

Phone: +34 928 46 78 54

Price Range: €50 - €100 per night

Hotel Aloe Canteras is a gem located right on Las Canteras Beach. It's perfect for budget travelers who still want a prime location. My room was simple but clean and comfortable, and I loved waking up to the sound of the waves. The rooftop terrace is a great spot for a morning coffee or an evening drink, offering panoramic views of the beach and the city.

2. RK Luz Playa Suites

Address: Calle Sagasta, 66, 35008 Las Palmas de Gran Canaria, Las Palmas

Phone: +34 928 22 41 82

Price Range: €60 - €120 per night

Another fantastic budget option is RK Luz Playa Suites. The suites are spacious and come with a kitchenette, which is great if you prefer to prepare some of your own meals. I stayed here for a week, and it felt like a home away from home. The location is unbeatable, just steps away from Las Canteras Beach, and there are plenty of restaurants and shops nearby.

Best for Families

Traveling with family can be a blast, especially when you have the right accommodations. Gran Canaria offers many family-friendly hotels that cater to the needs of both adults and kids.

1. Lopesan Baobab Resort

Address: Mar Adriático, 1, 35100 Meloneras, Las Palmas

Phone: +34 928 15 40 00

Price Range: €200 - €350 per night

The Lopesan Baobab Resort is a family favorite for good reason. The African-themed decor is unique and fascinating, and the resort boasts several pools, including ones specifically designed for children. My kids loved the water slides and the daily entertainment programs. The rooms are spacious enough for families, and the staff goes above and beyond to make sure everyone is happy. There's even a kids' club that gave us adults some much-needed downtime.

2. Gloria Palace Amadores Thalasso & Hotel

Address: Calle La Palma, 2, 35139 Amadores, Las Palmas

Phone: +34 928 12 85 28

Price Range: €150 - €250 per night

The Gloria Palace Amadores is perched on a cliff with stunning views of the Atlantic Ocean. The hotel features a large infinity pool and direct access to a beautiful beach. My family enjoyed the spacious rooms and the variety of activities offered, including a mini-golf course and a kids' playground. The Thalasso Spa is one of the best I've visited, and it was a treat to unwind while the kids were entertained.

Best for Couples

Gran Canaria is a romantic paradise, perfect for couples looking to spend some quality time together. Here are my top picks for the best hotels for couples.

1. Radisson Blu Resort & Spa, Gran Canaria

Address: Barranco de la Verga, s/n, 35120 Arguineguín, Las Palmas

Phone: +34 928 15 29 01

Price Range: €250 - €400 per night

The Radisson Blu Resort & Spa is a haven for couples. The rooms are luxurious, and many come with private balconies offering breathtaking ocean views. My partner and I spent a lot of time at the spa, which offers an extensive range of treatments. We also enjoyed romantic dinners at the on-site restaurant, which serves delicious Mediterranean cuisine. The resort's location is perfect for exploring nearby beaches and towns.

2. Marina Suites Gran Canaria

Address: Calle Juan Diaz Rodriguez, 10, 35130 Puerto Rico, Las Palmas

Phone: +34 928 15 28 43

Price Range: €180 - €300 per night

Marina Suites is ideal for couples seeking a mix of relaxation and adventure. The suites are spacious and beautifully decorated, with stunning views of the marina. We loved the infinity pool and the tranquil atmosphere. The staff was incredibly helpful, offering great recommendations for nearby restaurants and activities. A sunset boat tour organized by the hotel was a highlight of our trip.

Using Google Maps to Find Locations

Finding your way around Gran Canaria is a breeze with Google Maps. Here's how to use it to fetch the addresses listed from your current location:

Open Google Maps: On your smartphone or computer, open the Google Maps app or go to the Google Maps website.

Search for the Location: Enter the name or address of the place you're looking for in the search bar. For example, type "Seaside Grand Hotel Residencia."

Get Directions: Click on the location to open its details. You'll see options for directions. Click or tap on "Directions."

Enter Your Current Location: By default, Google Maps uses your current location if you have location services enabled. If not, you can manually enter your starting point.

Choose Your Mode of Transport: Select whether you're traveling by car, public transport, walking, or biking. Google Maps will provide the best route and estimated travel time.

Follow the Directions: Google Maps will guide you turn-by-turn to your destination. You can also save the directions for offline use if you're worried about data usage or connectivity.

Gran Canaria is a diverse and beautiful island with so much to offer, no matter what kind of traveler you are. Whether you're looking for luxury, traveling on a budget, taking a family trip, or enjoying a romantic getaway, there's the perfect place waiting for you. I hope this guide helps you find the perfect accommodation and adds to your incredible experience on this amazing island. Enjoy your stay, and don't forget to explore all the wonderful sights and activities Gran Canaria has to offer!

Chapter 13

Choosing the Right Accommodation for You

Factors to Consider

When planning a trip to Gran Canaria, finding the right place to stay can make all the difference in your experience. I remember the first time I visited the island; I was overwhelmed by the variety of accommodation options available. Whether you're looking for luxury, budget-friendly spots, or something unique, here are some factors to consider when choosing your perfect home away from home.

Budget

Let's face it, budget plays a huge role in deciding where to stay. Gran Canaria offers everything from five-star resorts to cozy guesthouses and affordable hostels. I found that setting a realistic budget helped narrow down my choices significantly. For luxury, you might consider the Seaside Grand Hotel Residencia in Maspalomas, which can run you around €400 per night. On the other end, there are charming hostels in Las Palmas, like HiTide House, costing around €25 per night for a dorm bed.

Location

Gran Canaria has diverse regions, each offering something unique. If you love the hustle and bustle, Las Palmas de Gran Canaria, the island's capital, is the place to be. I loved wandering through Vegueta, the old town, with its cobblestone streets and historic buildings. Staying here also meant I was close to urban beaches like Las Canteras. On the other hand, Maspalomas and Playa del Inglés in the south are perfect if you're after stunning beaches and vibrant nightlife. For a quieter, more local vibe, consider areas like Agaete or Puerto de Mogán.

Amenities

Depending on your needs, the amenities offered by your accommodation can significantly impact your stay. I always look for places with reliable Wi-Fi because I love sharing my travel experiences online. If you're planning a romantic getaway, a resort with a spa, like the Lopesan Villa del Conde Resort & Thalasso, might be ideal. Families might prefer places with kitchen facilities or kids' clubs. For example, Cordial Mogan Playa in Puerto de Mogán offers family-friendly amenities and a beautiful garden.

Location and Amenities

Let's dive a bit deeper into what each area of Gran Canaria has to offer and the amenities you might find beneficial during your stay.

Las Palmas de Gran Canaria

Staying in Las Palmas puts you at the heart of the action. I stayed at Hotel Reina Isabel, right on Las Canteras Beach. Waking up to the sound of the waves was magical. This hotel, at C/ Alfredo L. Jones, 40, 35008 Las Palmas de Gran Canaria, also had a rooftop pool with breathtaking views. Prices here range from €120 to €250 per night.

The city's public transport is excellent, and having a car isn't necessary unless you plan to explore the island extensively. Las Palmas also has a great selection of restaurants, shops, and cultural sites. Don't miss out on the Sunday market in Vegueta and the fantastic tapas at La Marinera, just a stone's throw from the beach.

Maspalomas and Playa del Inglés

If you're a beach lover, the southern coast is where you'll want to be. I once stayed at the Seaside Palm Beach in Maspalomas, known for its luxurious amenities and proximity to the famous dunes. The address is Av. del Oasis, 32, 35100 Maspalomas, and prices range from €200 to €350 per night. The hotel's spa was a perfect way to unwind after a day exploring the dunes.

Playa del Inglés is famous for its nightlife. Staying at the AxelBeach Maspalomas, an adults-only hotel located at Av. de Tirajana, 32, 35100 Playa del Inglés, was a great choice for being close to the action.

Rooms here start at €100 per night, and the hotel features a fantastic pool and wellness area.

Puerto de Mogán

Known as "Little Venice," Puerto de Mogán is perfect for a romantic stay. I stayed at Hotel Cordial Mogán Playa, located at Av. los Marrero, 2, 35138 Puerto de Mogán. This hotel's lush gardens and charming architecture made it feel like a hidden paradise. Prices range from €150 to €250 per night. The hotel also offers diving courses, which was a fun way to explore the marine life.

Agaete

For a more tranquil experience, consider Agaete. I stayed at the Hotel & Spa Cordial Roca Negra, which offered stunning views of the ocean and was perfect for a quiet retreat. The address is Av. Alfredo Kraus, 42, 35480 Agaete, and rooms range from €80 to €150 per night. The hotel's proximity to the natural swimming pools of Las Salinas was a highlight.

Reviews and Recommendations

Reading reviews and getting recommendations can provide invaluable insights. Here are some personal experiences and tips to help you decide.

Luxury Resorts

For a luxury stay, I highly recommend the Seaside Grand Hotel Residencia. My experience here was unforgettable. The service was impeccable, and the amenities were top-notch. Located at Av. del Oasis, 32, 35100 Maspalomas, this hotel is perfect for those looking to indulge. Prices are around €400 per night, but it's worth every penny for the luxurious experience.

Budget-Friendly Hotels

If you're traveling on a budget, HiTide House in Las Palmas is a fantastic option. This hostel has a friendly atmosphere and is just a minute's walk from Las Canteras Beach. The address is Calle Fernando Guanarteme, 27, 35010 Las Palmas de Gran Canaria, and beds are around €25 per night. The rooftop terrace was a great spot to meet fellow travelers and enjoy the sunset.

Boutique Guesthouses

For a unique and intimate stay, consider the Old Chocolate Factory in Las Palmas. This guesthouse, located at Calle Hernán Pérez de Grado, 24, 35001 Las Palmas de Gran Canaria, combines history with modern comfort. Prices range from €80 to €120 per night. I loved the personalized touch and the charming decor that made it feel like a home away from home.

Unique Stays

If you're looking for something different, try staying in a cave house in Artenara. I stayed at Casa-Cueva El Mimo, which was a unique experience. The address is Calle Las Arvejas, 2, 35350 Artenara, and prices start at €70 per night. The cave's natural insulation kept it cool in the summer, and the views of the surrounding mountains were breathtaking.

Booking Tips and Tricks

Booking the right accommodation can save you time, money, and stress. Here are some tips based on my experiences.

Best Times to Book

Booking in advance, especially during peak seasons, can ensure you get the best rates and availability. I usually book my stays 3-6 months ahead. For off-peak travel, last-minute deals can offer significant savings. For instance, I found a great deal at the Radisson Blu Resort in Puerto de Mogán by booking just two weeks in advance.

Finding Deals and Discounts

Always compare prices across multiple booking platforms. Websites like Booking.com, Expedia, and Agoda often have different rates and promotions. I once saved 20% on my stay at the Hotel Riu Palace Meloneras by booking through their official website during a promotional period.

Using Booking Platforms

Sign up for newsletters and loyalty programs. Many hotels offer exclusive discounts to subscribers. I joined the loyalty program for Lopesan Hotels and enjoyed benefits like free upgrades and late check-outs during my stay at the Lopesan Baobab Resort.

Final Thoughts

Choosing the right accommodation is more than just finding a place to sleep; it's about enhancing your overall experience in Gran Canaria. From the bustling streets of Las Palmas to the serene beaches of Puerto de Mogán, there's something for every traveler. Remember to consider your budget, preferred location, and desired amenities. Reading reviews and getting personal recommendations can also guide you to the best options. Whether you're looking for luxury, budget-friendly spots, or something unique, Gran Canaria has it all.

I hope my experiences and tips help you find the perfect place to stay and make your visit to Gran Canaria unforgettable. Enjoy your travels!

Chapter 14

Booking Tips and Tricks

Booking your trip to Gran Canaria can be an exciting process, but it can also be a bit daunting with so many options available. Having spent a considerable amount of time exploring this beautiful island, I've gathered some tips and tricks to help you make the most of your booking experience. From the best times to book to finding deals and discounts, and using booking platforms effectively, let me share my personal experiences and insights with you.

Best Times to Book

When it comes to booking your trip to Gran Canaria, timing is everything. The island enjoys a subtropical climate, making it a year-round destination. However, there are specific times when booking can be more advantageous.

High Season vs. Low Season

Gran Canaria's high season typically runs from November to April, coinciding with the winter months in Europe. During this time, the island is bustling with tourists looking to escape the cold. I remember my first winter trip to Gran Canaria – the beaches were lively, the streets filled with music and laughter, and every corner seemed to promise a new adventure. However, with this surge in visitors comes higher prices for flights and accommodations. If you're planning to visit during this period, it's best to book well in advance, ideally six months prior, to secure the best rates.

The low season, on the other hand, is from May to October. This period includes the hot summer months when the island sees fewer tourists. The weather can be quite hot, especially in July and August, but this also means that flights and accommodations are generally cheaper. I once visited in early September and found the island to be delightfully quiet, with plenty of space on the beaches and no long waits at restaurants. Booking two to three months in advance during the low season can often yield excellent deals.

Shoulder Seasons

The shoulder seasons, May-June and September-October, are my personal favorites. The weather is still pleasant, and the crowds are more manageable. These months offer a perfect balance between affordability and comfort. I've found that booking around three to four months in advance during the shoulder seasons can often result in significant savings.

Finding Deals and Discounts

Who doesn't love a good deal? Over the years, I've picked up a few strategies to help stretch my travel budget further.

Sign Up for Newsletters

One of the easiest ways to stay informed about deals and discounts is to sign up for newsletters from airlines and travel agencies. I'm subscribed to several, and I can't count the number of times I've received exclusive discounts or early access to sales. For instance, I once snagged a round-trip ticket from London to Gran Canaria for just €150 during a flash sale announced via a newsletter. It pays to be in the know!

Use Price Comparison Websites

Websites like Skyscanner, Momondo, and Google Flights are invaluable tools for comparing prices across different airlines and booking platforms. I always start my search here to get a sense of the price range and identify the cheapest options. A tip I've learned is to set up price alerts on these sites – they'll notify you when prices drop, helping you to catch deals as soon as they appear.

Flexible Dates and Locations

Flexibility can be a significant advantage when booking. If your travel dates are flexible, use the "flexible dates" option on flight search engines. This feature allows you to compare prices over a range of dates and choose the most economical option. Similarly, being flexible with your departure airport can sometimes lead to substantial savings. On one occasion, flying out from a smaller regional airport instead of a major hub saved me over €100.

Loyalty Programs and Credit Card Rewards

If you travel frequently, joining airline loyalty programs can be very beneficial. Accumulating miles can lead to free flights, upgrades, and other perks. I'm a member of a few programs and always try to book flights with airlines where I can earn miles. Additionally, using credit cards that offer travel rewards can help you accumulate points that can be redeemed for flights, hotels, and more. Just last year, I redeemed points for a three-night stay at a lovely boutique hotel in Las Palmas.

Using Booking Platforms

Booking platforms have revolutionized the way we travel, offering a wide range of options at our fingertips. However, navigating these platforms can sometimes be tricky. Here are some of my personal tips for using them effectively.

Popular Booking Platforms

Websites like Booking.com, Expedia, and Airbnb are among my go-to platforms for booking accommodations. They offer a variety of options, from luxury resorts to budget-friendly guesthouses. When using these sites, always read reviews and check ratings – they can provide valuable insights into what to expect. For example, during my last trip, I found a charming bed and breakfast on Booking.com with rave reviews about its breakfast spread, and it did not disappoint!

Direct Booking vs. Third-Party Sites

While third-party booking sites offer convenience and sometimes better rates, booking directly with hotels can also have its advantages. Many hotels offer price match guarantees, exclusive perks, or loyalty points when you book directly through their website. I once booked directly with a hotel and received a free room upgrade and complimentary breakfast, which wouldn't have been available through a third-party site.

Using Filters and Sorting Options

When searching for accommodations, use the filters and sorting options to narrow down your choices. Whether you're looking for a beachfront property, a place with a pool, or pet-friendly accommodations, these filters can help you find exactly what you're looking for. Sorting by price, distance from the city center, or guest rating can also streamline your search. On my first trip to Gran Canaria, I used the "beachfront" filter and discovered a gem of a hotel right on Playa de las Canteras.

Reading the Fine Print

Always read the fine print before making a booking. Cancellation policies, additional fees, and check-in/check-out times can vary significantly between properties. During one trip, I nearly booked a non-refundable room by mistake. Thankfully, I caught it in time and opted for a slightly more expensive room with free cancellation, which turned out to be a lifesaver when my plans changed last minute.

Contacting the Property

If you have specific requirements or questions, don't hesitate to contact the property directly. This can be particularly useful if you need an early check-in, a late check-out, or special accommodations. I've found that most properties are very accommodating when you reach out directly. For instance, when traveling with my elderly parents, I contacted our hotel in advance to arrange for a ground-floor room and received prompt and helpful responses.

Local Agencies

Sometimes, local travel agencies can offer better deals and more personalized service. In Gran Canaria, there are several reputable agencies that can help you find accommodations, plan excursions, and even arrange transportation. During one of my trips, I used the services of a local agency, and they arranged an amazing itinerary that included a guided hike in the Tamadaba Natural Park and a boat tour along the coast.

Avoiding Scams

While booking online, be cautious of potential scams. Always use reputable websites and check for secure payment options. If something seems too good to be true, it probably is. I remember a friend who almost booked a stunning villa at an unbelievably low price, only to find out it was a scam. Trust your instincts and do your research.

Practical Booking Tips

Booking Flights

When booking flights, consider the following tips to make your journey smoother and more affordable:

Book Early: As mentioned earlier, booking in advance can often secure better rates, especially during peak travel seasons.

Choose the Right Seat: For long-haul flights, choosing the right seat can make a significant difference in comfort. Websites like SeatGuru provide detailed seating charts and reviews for various airlines.

Check Baggage Policies: Airlines have different baggage policies, and additional baggage fees can add up quickly. Make sure to check these policies before booking.

Booking Accommodations

When booking accommodations, keep these tips in mind:

Check Amenities: Ensure that the property has all the amenities you need for a comfortable stay. I always look for Wi-Fi, air conditioning, and breakfast options.

Look for Deals: Many booking platforms offer deals and discounts, especially if you're a frequent user or a member of their loyalty program. I've often found "Genius" discounts on Booking.com, which saved me a good amount on my stays.

Consider Location: The location of your accommodation can greatly impact your experience. Staying in the city center or near major attractions can save you time and transportation costs. However, sometimes staying a bit further out can provide a more authentic experience and be more budget-friendly.

Booking Activities and Excursions

To make the most of your time in Gran Canaria, consider pre-booking some activities and excursions:

Research in Advance: Look up popular tours and activities and read reviews to find the best options. Websites like TripAdvisor and Viator can be very helpful.

Book Early for Popular Attractions: For popular attractions like Palmitos Park or guided tours in the Maspalomas Dunes, booking in advance can ensure you get a spot and sometimes even a better rate.

Local Guides: Hiring a local guide can provide you with a deeper understanding of the area and its culture. During one of my trips, I booked a walking tour of Las Palmas with a local guide, and it was one of the highlights of my visit.

Booking your trip to Gran Canaria doesn't have to be stressful. With a little planning and these tips, you can secure the best deals and make your trip as smooth and enjoyable as possible. Happy travels!

Useful Contacts:

Gran Canaria Airport (LPA)

Address: Autopista GC-1, s/n, 35230, Las Palmas, Spain

Phone: +34 928 579 000

Chapter 15

Culinary Delights of Gran Canaria

Exploring the culinary landscape of Gran Canaria is like embarking on a flavorful adventure. This island, with its rich cultural heritage, offers a gastronomic experience that's as diverse as its landscapes. From traditional Canarian dishes to innovative modern cuisine, there's something to satisfy every palate. Having spent a delightful amount of time here, let me take you through some of the culinary gems I've discovered.

Must-Try Dishes

One of the first things I did when I arrived in Gran Canaria was to dive into the local cuisine. Here are some must-try dishes that you absolutely cannot miss.

Papas Arrugadas con Mojo (Wrinkled Potatoes with Mojo Sauce): This is a quintessential Canarian dish.

The small, wrinkled potatoes are boiled in salted water until they have a wonderfully salty crust, and they're served with two types of mojo sauce – red (mojo rojo) and green (mojo verde). The sauces are a blend of garlic, olive oil, vinegar, and spices, and they add a tangy kick to the potatoes.

Sancocho Canario: A traditional fish stew that's both hearty and comforting. It's made with salted fish, usually wreckfish, which is then boiled with potatoes, sweet potatoes, and served with mojo sauce. This dish is a perfect representation of the island's seafaring traditions.

Gofio: This ancient grain product, made from roasted corn or wheat flour, is a staple in Canarian cuisine. It can be added to soups, mixed with milk for breakfast, or used in desserts. It has a nutty flavor that's quite unique.

Bienmesabe: For those with a sweet tooth, this dessert is a must-try. It's made from ground almonds, honey, sugar, and egg yolks, creating a rich and sweet paste often served with ice cream.

These dishes are not just meals; they are a journey into the history and culture of the Canary Islands. Each bite tells a story of the island's heritage, and the flavors are as vibrant as the scenery.

Top Restaurants

Finding the perfect place to eat can sometimes be overwhelming, especially with so many great options. Here are some top restaurants that I highly recommend.

Restaurante El Centro

Calle León y Castillo, 21, Las Palmas

Phone: +34 928 36 54 89

El Centro offers a fantastic blend of traditional Canarian and modern Spanish cuisine. Their seafood paella is a highlight, and the ambiance is perfect for a relaxed evening meal. I still remember the taste of their fresh octopus salad – it was absolutely divine.

La Aquarela

Avenida Los Marrero, 35, Patalavaca

Phone: +34 928 15 76 43

La Aquarela is a fine dining experience that should not be missed. It's a bit on the pricier side, with main courses averaging around €30-€40, but the exquisite dishes and stunning ocean views make it worth every cent. Their tasting menu is a culinary journey that showcases the best of local ingredients and flavors.

El Equilibrista 33

Calle Simancas, 33, Las Palmas

Phone: +34 928 92 18 26

This restaurant is known for its innovative approach to traditional dishes. The chef's creative flair shines through in every dish. I had the roasted suckling pig, and it was cooked to perfection – crispy on the outside and tender on the inside.

La Marinera

Paseo de las Canteras, s/n, Las Palmas

Phone: +34 928 46 30 60

Located right on the beach, La Marinera offers fresh seafood with a view. It's the perfect place to enjoy a leisurely lunch after a morning swim. Their grilled sardines and Canarian-style fish are highly recommended.

Cafés and Bakeries

Gran Canaria's café culture is vibrant and welcoming. Whether you're looking for a quick coffee or a place to linger with a pastry, there are plenty of charming spots to choose from.

Café Regina

Calle Sagasta, 63, Las Palmas

Phone: +34 928 27 28 29

Café Regina is my go-to spot for a morning coffee. They serve a variety of brews, from espresso to cortado, and their pastries are simply irresistible. The almond croissant is a personal favorite, and at just €2.50, it's a steal.

Panadería Mis Hijos

Avenida de Canarias, 305, Vecindario

Phone: +34 928 75 12 34

This family-run bakery offers a delightful array of breads and pastries. Their gofio bread is a local specialty, and the chocolate-filled pastries are a hit with everyone. It's a great place to grab a quick breakfast or snack.

Dulcería Nublo

Calle Real de la Plaza, 5, Tejeda

Phone: +34 928 66 62 27

Located in the picturesque village of Tejeda, Dulcería Nublo is famous for its traditional Canarian sweets. Their almond cakes and bienmesabe are perfect for satisfying a sweet tooth. The prices are reasonable, with most treats costing between €1 and €3.

Mr. Kale

Calle Ruiz de Alda, 24, Las Palmas

Phone: +34 928 92 07 11

For a healthier option, Mr. Kale offers a range of smoothies, salads, and vegan pastries. It's a great place to refuel after exploring the city. Their avocado toast is a must-try, and it's priced at €7.

Tapas Bars

No visit to Spain would be complete without indulging in some tapas, and Gran Canaria has some fantastic spots to enjoy these small plates.

Tapas Locas

Calle Mendizábal, 27, Las Palmas

Phone: +34 928 31 21 34

Tapas Locas is a lively place with a great atmosphere. The variety of tapas is impressive, and the flavors are bold. I recommend the garlic prawns and patatas bravas. The prices are reasonable, with most tapas ranging from €3 to €5.

La Bodeguita de Medio

Calle Sagasta, 66, Las Palmas

Phone: +34 928 27 44 56

This cozy tapas bar offers a more traditional experience. The jamón ibérico and chorizo are delicious, and the wine selection is excellent. It's a great spot to unwind with friends over a glass of wine and some tasty bites.

El Rinconcito de Telde

Calle Constantino, 5, Telde

Phone: +34 928 70 23 12

El Rinconcito de Telde is a hidden gem. The tapas are freshly made and the service is friendly. The grilled octopus and Spanish tortilla are particularly good. It's a bit off the beaten path, but well worth the visit.

Bar La Cueva

Calle Mayor de Triana, 87, Las Palmas

Phone: +34 928 37 22 11

Bar La Cueva is a great spot for tapas in the heart of Las Palmas. The ambiance is casual and welcoming, and the food is consistently good. I love their meatballs in almond sauce and the croquettes. Prices are very reasonable, with most dishes under €5.

Exploring the culinary delights of Gran Canaria has been one of the highlights of my travels. Each meal is an opportunity to connect with the local culture and traditions. From savoring fresh seafood by the beach to enjoying a leisurely coffee in a charming café, the island offers a diverse and delicious dining experience that will leave you wanting more. So, whether you're a foodie looking for the next great meal or just someone who enjoys good food, Gran Canaria has something to offer. Bon appétit!

Chapter 16

Day Trips and Excursions in Gran Canaria

Nearby Towns and Villages

Agaete and Puerto de las Nieves

If you're looking for a day trip that combines charming town vibes with stunning coastal scenery, Agaete and its port, Puerto de las Nieves, should be at the top of your list. Agaete, located in the northwest of Gran Canaria, is a quaint village with white-washed houses and narrow streets that beg to be explored. I remember my first visit there; it felt like stepping back in time.

The town's most famous attraction is the Huerto de las Flores, a beautiful botanical garden with a collection of exotic plants and flowers. It's the perfect place to relax and enjoy nature. Entrance is about €3, and it's open from 10 AM to 6 PM daily. You can find it at Calle de las Huertas, 6, 35480 Agaete.

Just a short walk from the town center is Puerto de las Nieves, a picturesque fishing port. The crystal-clear waters and dramatic cliffs are breathtaking. The seafood here is unbeatable; I had the most delicious grilled octopus at a local restaurant called Dedo de Dios (Calle de la Concepción, 10, 35480 Puerto de las Nieves). Their phone number is +34 928 88 00 96, and a meal will set you back around €25.

Teror

Another delightful town to visit is Teror, located in the northern part of the island. Known for its traditional Canarian architecture, Teror is a perfect destination for a leisurely day trip. The town is famous for its wooden balconies and the Basilica of Nuestra Señora del Pino, which is a must-visit. I was lucky to be there during the annual Fiesta del Pino, held in September, which celebrates the town's patron saint. The streets were filled with music, dancing, and food stalls—truly a festive experience.

For lunch, I highly recommend Casa del Pino, located at Plaza de Nuestra Señora del Pino, 6, 35330 Teror. Their phone number is +34 928 61 90 23. The place serves authentic Canarian dishes; try their potaje de berros (watercress soup) for about €10.

Natural Wonders

Bandama Caldera

Gran Canaria's volcanic origins have gifted it with some incredible natural wonders. One of my favorite day trips was to the Bandama Caldera, a massive volcanic crater about 20 minutes from Las Palmas. The caldera is around 1,000 meters in diameter and 200 meters deep, making it a striking sight.

You can hike down into the caldera, which is an amazing experience. The trail is well-marked and takes about an hour to descend and another hour to climb back up. I recommend starting early in the morning to avoid the midday heat. The views from the top are spectacular, offering a panoramic vista of the surrounding landscapes.

Nearby is the Bandama Golf Course, the oldest golf course in Spain, which offers a great spot to relax after your hike. The golf course is located at Carretera de Bandama, s/n, 35310 Santa Brígida. You can contact them at +34 928 35 00 00. Green fees start at €60.

Roque Nublo

Another must-see natural wonder is Roque Nublo, an iconic volcanic rock that stands proudly in the center of the island. The drive to the base of the rock takes you through winding mountain roads with stunning views at every turn. Once you arrive, it's a moderate hike of about 1.5 kilometers to reach the rock itself.

Standing at the foot of Roque Nublo, I felt a profound sense of awe. The rock is surrounded by pine forests and offers incredible views of the island. On a clear day, you can even see the neighboring island of Tenerife and its famous Mount Teide.

The best time to visit is either early morning or late afternoon to catch the sunrise or sunset. There's a small café at the parking area where you can grab a coffee before or after your hike. It's located at GC-600, 35369 Tejeda, and their phone number is +34 928 66 63 00.

Cultural Excursions

Arucas

For those interested in culture and history, Arucas is a fantastic destination. This town is known for its impressive neo-Gothic church, Iglesia de San Juan Bautista, often referred to as the Arucas Cathedral, though it's technically not a cathedral. The church's intricate design and towering spires are stunning. I spent a good hour just admiring the architecture and taking photos.

Arucas is also famous for its rum. The Arehucas Rum Distillery, located at Calle Era de San Pedro, 2, 35400 Arucas, offers guided tours where you can learn about the rum-making process and sample different varieties. The tour costs about €7, and it's well worth it. Their contact number is +34 928 62 25 35.

Gáldar

Gáldar, located in the north of Gran Canaria, is another cultural gem. The town is home to the Cueva Pintada Museum and Archaeological Park, which showcases ancient Canarian cave paintings. The museum offers a fascinating glimpse into the island's pre-Hispanic history. Entrance is €6, and it's open from 10 AM to 6 PM. You can find it at Calle Audiencia, 2, 35460 Gáldar, and their phone number is +34 928 89 54 89.

After visiting the museum, take a stroll through Gáldar's charming town center. I enjoyed a wonderful meal at La Pizarra, a local restaurant located at Plaza de Santiago, 3, 35460 Gáldar. Their phone number is +34 928 88 04 22. The roasted pork with mojo sauce was unforgettable and reasonably priced at €15.

Tejeda

Tejeda, located in the heart of the island, is a picturesque village known for its almond trees and traditional Canarian pastries. The drive to Tejeda offers some of the most breathtaking views of the island's mountainous interior. Once you arrive, make sure to visit the Dulcería Nublo, located at Calle Dr. Domingo Hernández Guerra, 8, 35360 Tejeda. Their phone number is +34 928 66 63 75. They serve delicious almond-based sweets, perfect for a mid-morning snack.

Tejeda is also a great base for exploring the surrounding mountains. The nearby Cruz de Tejeda is a popular starting point for several hiking trails that offer stunning panoramic views. Don't miss the Parador de Cruz de Tejeda, a beautiful hotel and restaurant with a terrace that overlooks the mountains. It's located at Cruz de Tejeda, s/n, 35328 Tejeda, and their phone number is +34 928 01 73 00. A meal here costs around €30, and the views alone are worth the price.

Maspalomas Dunes

No visit to Gran Canaria is complete without experiencing the Maspalomas Dunes. This unique natural reserve offers a desert-like landscape right next to the ocean. Walking through the dunes, I felt like I was on another planet. The best way to explore the area is on foot or by camel. Camel rides are available for about €15 and offer a fun and unique perspective of the dunes.

The Maspalomas Lighthouse, located at Plaza del Faro, 15, 35100 Maspalomas, is another must-see in the area. The lighthouse has been guiding ships since 1890 and provides a beautiful backdrop for photos. There's also a small museum inside that details the history of the lighthouse and the region. Entry is free, and it's open from 10 AM to 5 PM.

After exploring the dunes and the lighthouse, head to Meloneras, a nearby upscale area with great shopping and dining options. I had a fantastic dinner at La Proa Casa Reyes, located at Av. del Oasis, 26, 35100 Meloneras. Their phone number is +34 928 14 31 12.

The seafood paella is a must-try, costing about €20 per person.

Puerto de Mogán

Often referred to as "Little Venice," Puerto de Mogán is a picturesque fishing village on the southwest coast of Gran Canaria. The village is known for its charming canals, whitewashed buildings, and vibrant bougainvillea. I spent a delightful afternoon wandering through the narrow streets and taking in the serene atmosphere.

Puerto de Mogán also has a fantastic beach, perfect for a relaxing swim or sunbathing. The waters are calm and clear, making it ideal for families with children. There are plenty of beachfront restaurants where you can enjoy a meal with a view. I recommend Restaurante Olivia, located at Urbanización Puerto de Mogán, s/n, 35138 Mogán. Their phone number is +34 928 56 51 45. The grilled fish of the day is excellent and costs around €18.

On Fridays, Puerto de Mogán hosts a lively market where you can buy everything from local crafts to fresh produce. It's a great place to pick up souvenirs and enjoy the vibrant atmosphere. The market runs from 9 AM to 2 PM, and it's best to arrive early to avoid the crowds.

Fataga

Nestled in the Fataga Ravine, this charming village offers a glimpse into traditional Canarian life. The drive to Fataga, known as the Valley of a Thousand Palms, is incredibly scenic, with lush greenery and dramatic cliffs. Upon arriving, I was struck by the village's tranquility and the beauty of its traditional houses.

One of the highlights of my visit was the Centro de Interpretación del Barranco de Fataga, an interpretive center that provides insights into the region's history and natural environment. It's located at Calle León y Castillo, 6, 35108 Fataga, and their phone number is +34 928 72 34 56. The entrance fee is €4.

For lunch, I dined at El Albaricoque, a cozy restaurant offering delicious local dishes. It's located at Calle San Jose, 5, 35108 Fataga, and their phone number is +34 928 17 35 40. The rabbit stew is a local specialty and costs about €12.

Santa Lucia de Tirajana

This town, situated in the heart of Gran Canaria, is known for its stunning landscapes and historical sites. The Fortaleza de Ansite, an ancient fortress offering panoramic views of the surrounding area, is a must-visit. The entrance fee is €5, and it's located at Calle la Sorrueda, 1, 35280 Santa Lucia de Tirajana. Their phone number is +34 928 16 12 54.

The town's main square, Plaza de Santa Lucia, is a great place to relax and soak in the local atmosphere. There are several cafes where you can enjoy a coffee and watch the world go by. I particularly enjoyed a visit to Dulcería Nublo, located at Plaza de Santa Lucia, 4, 35280 Santa Lucia de Tirajana. Their phone number is +34 928 16 13 75. They serve fantastic pastries for about €3 each.

For a bit of adventure, head to the nearby La Sorrueda Dam, where you can hike and enjoy the beautiful scenery. The dam is located about 5 kilometers from the town center and offers several trails with varying difficulty levels.

In conclusion, Gran Canaria offers an incredible array of day trips and excursions that cater to all interests, whether you're a history buff, a nature enthusiast, or someone simply looking to relax and enjoy the island's beauty. Each destination provides a unique glimpse into the island's rich culture and diverse landscapes, making every trip an unforgettable experience. So, pack your bags, plan your itinerary, and get ready to explore the wonders of Gran Canaria!

Chapter 17

When to Visit Gran Canaria

Best Seasons and Weather

When planning your trip to Gran Canaria, timing can make all the difference in your experience. I've been lucky enough to visit this beautiful island at various times of the year, and each season has its unique charm.

Spring (March to May): Spring is one of my favorite times to visit Gran Canaria. The weather is pleasantly warm, with temperatures ranging from 20°C to 24°C (68°F to 75°F). The island is lush and green after the winter rains, making it perfect for outdoor activities like hiking and exploring the scenic trails. Plus, the crowds are relatively thin, so you can enjoy popular spots without feeling overwhelmed. One spring, I spent a delightful afternoon wandering through the Jardín Botánico Viera y Clavijo (Botanical Garden), located in Tafira Alta. The entrance fee is around €1.50, and it's open daily from 9:00 AM to 6:00 PM.

Trust me, the vibrant flora in full bloom is a sight to behold.

Summer (June to August): If you love the sun and can handle the heat, summer in Gran Canaria is your season. Temperatures soar to between 25°C and 30°C (77°F to 86°F), perfect for beach lovers and water sports enthusiasts. The beaches, such as Playa de Amadores and Playa del Inglés, are buzzing with activity. Just remember to bring plenty of sunscreens! One summer, I took a windsurfing lesson at Pozo Izquierdo. The windsurfing school, Cutre (Calle el Ancla, 2, 35100 Pozo Izquierdo), offers lessons starting at €50 per hour. Their phone number is +34 928 79 91 73. It was exhilarating to glide over the waves, and I highly recommend it.

Autumn (September to November): Autumn is another fantastic time to visit. The temperatures are slightly cooler, ranging from 22°C to 27°C (72°F to 81°F), and the summer crowds have thinned out. This is an excellent time for exploring the island's cultural and historical sites. I recall a memorable visit to the Cueva Pintada Museum and Archaeological Park in

Gáldar during October. The guided tour costs around €6, and it's worth every penny to see the ancient cave paintings. You can contact them at +34 928 89 54 89 for more information.

Winter (December to February): Winter in Gran Canaria is mild and quite pleasant compared to the rest of Europe. Temperatures range from 18°C to 22°C (64°F to 72°F), making it an ideal winter sun destination. I spent a magical Christmas in Las Palmas de Gran Canaria, enjoying the festive lights and local traditions. The city's main shopping street, Calle Triana, was beautifully decorated, and the Christmas market at Plaza de Santa Catalina was a joy to explore. Don't miss the "Belén de Arena" (Sand Nativity) on Las Canteras Beach, a unique and impressive display. Admission is free, but donations are welcome.

Key Events and Festivals

Gran Canaria hosts a variety of events and festivals throughout the year, each offering a glimpse into the island's rich culture and traditions. Here are some that I've had the pleasure of experiencing:

Carnival (February to March): The Gran Canaria Carnival is one of the most vibrant and lively events on the island. Held in Las Palmas, this festival is a riot of color, music, and dance. I remember joining the festivities in 2019, dressed in a flamboyant costume, dancing through the streets with locals and tourists alike. The highlight was the Drag Queen Gala, a spectacular show of creativity and flair. If you're planning to attend, book your accommodation early, as the city gets packed. For more details, you can contact the Carnival office at +34 928 44 60 00.

Fiestas de San Juan (June 24th): This festival marks the summer solstice and is celebrated with bonfires, fireworks, and beach parties. I celebrated San Juan at Las Canteras Beach, where we jumped over bonfires for good luck and watched the midnight fireworks light up the sky. It's a magical night, full of local customs and a fantastic way to immerse yourself in the island's culture.

Fiestas de la Virgen del Pino (September 8th): This is the main religious festival in Gran Canaria, held in Teror to honor the island's patron saint, the Virgin of the Pine. I visited Teror during the festival, and it was a heartwarming experience. The town was beautifully decorated, and the procession to the Basílica de Nuestra Señora del Pino was a moving spectacle. Teror is also known for its traditional Canarian architecture and charming streets. Don't forget to try the local delicacy, chorizo de Teror, a delicious spreadable sausage.

International Film Festival of Las Palmas (April): If you're a film enthusiast like me, you'll love this event. The festival showcases a diverse selection of international films, and it's a great opportunity to see some fantastic cinema. I attended a screening at the Teatro Pérez Galdós (Plaza Stagno, 1, 35002 Las Palmas de Gran Canaria) and was impressed by the quality of films and the enthusiasm of the audience. Tickets range from €4 to €6 per screening.

Off-Peak Travel Tips

Traveling to Gran Canaria during off-peak times can be a rewarding experience. Here are some tips based on my visits:

Take Advantage of Lower Prices: Off-peak seasons, particularly late autumn and early spring, often mean cheaper flights and accommodation. I scored a fantastic deal on a hotel in Puerto de Mogán in November. The Radisson Blu Resort & Spa, Gran Canaria Mogan (Av. Los Marreros, 35, 35138 Lomo Quiebre) had rooms for as low as €120 per night. Their phone number is +34 928 15 00 04. The town was quieter, and I had more space to enjoy the picturesque marina and charming streets.

Enjoy Less Crowded Attractions: Visiting popular attractions outside the peak tourist season means fewer crowds and a more relaxed experience. I visited the Maspalomas Dunes in early February, and it was a serene and tranquil walk through the sand dunes without the summer crowds. The silence and vastness of the dunes were truly meditative.

Pack Accordingly: Even during off-peak seasons, Gran Canaria's weather can be unpredictable. Bring layers, as evenings can get cooler, especially in the mountainous regions. On a January trip to the island's interior, I was glad to have my jacket while exploring the beautiful village of Tejeda, where the temperature can drop significantly at night.

Engage with Locals: With fewer tourists around, locals tend to be more relaxed and open to conversations. I had some of the best chats with residents during off-peak visits, learning about hidden spots and gaining insider tips. One evening in March, I struck up a conversation with the owner of a small tapas bar in Vegueta, Las Palmas. She recommended a hidden beach in the south that became a highlight of my trip.

Explore the Local Cuisine: Off-peak times are perfect for indulging in the local food scene without long waits. I enjoyed a delightful dinner at Restaurante La Aquarela (Apartamentos Aquamarina, Barranco de la Verga, 35120 Arguineguín), where a five-course tasting menu costs around €70. Their phone number is +34 928 73 04 42. The dishes, a modern take on traditional Canarian cuisine, were exquisite, and the service was impeccable.

Take Part in Unique Activities: Some activities and tours are more enjoyable when the island is less crowded. For instance, I took a guided stargazing tour in the highlands of Gran Canaria in October. The clear skies and absence of light pollution made for an unforgettable experience. The tour was organized by AstroGC (contact: +34 649 17 51 85) and cost €45 per person.

Visiting Gran Canaria is a delightful experience any time of the year, but understanding the seasons and planning your trip around them can enhance your visit significantly. Whether you're basking in the summer sun on a golden beach or exploring cultural festivals in the cooler months, Gran Canaria offers something special for every traveler. I hope these insights help you plan a trip that's as magical and memorable as mine have been.

Chapter 18

Health and Safety in Gran Canaria

Essential Health Tips

Hey there, fellow traveler! If you're planning to visit Gran Canaria, it's crucial to keep health and safety at the top of your list. Trust me, as someone who's been there, you want to be prepared so you can fully enjoy this beautiful island.

1. Hydration is Key

Gran Canaria's warm climate can be quite deceiving. Even if you're lounging on the beach or exploring the island's stunning landscapes, it's easy to get dehydrated. Always carry a bottle of water with you. Tap water is safe to drink, but bottled water is readily available and convenient. I remember one hot day exploring the dunes of Maspalomas, and boy, was I glad I had my trusty water bottle with me!

2. Sun Protection

The sun here can be intense, especially during the summer months. Don't forget to pack a high-SPF sunscreen and reapply it every couple of hours. A wide-brimmed hat and sunglasses are also essential to protect yourself from those powerful UV rays. One time, I got so caught up in the beauty of Playa de Amadores that I forgot to reapply sunscreen and ended up with a nasty sunburn. Learn from my mistake!

3. Local Cuisine and Food Safety

The food in Gran Canaria is delicious, with plenty of fresh seafood, fruits, and vegetables. While it's tempting to dive into every culinary delight, ensure that the food is properly cooked and that you wash any fresh produce before eating. Street food is safe to enjoy, but always choose stalls that look clean and have a good turnover of customers. I had some of the best tapas at a small market in Las Palmas – fresh, flavorful, and safe!

4. Insect Protection

Mosquitoes aren't a massive problem on the island, but it's better to be safe than sorry. Especially if you're venturing into more rural areas or nature parks, a good insect repellent will come in handy. Once, while hiking in the Tamadaba Natural Park, I was glad I had packed my repellent, as the bugs can be a bit bothersome in the evening.

5. Medical Facilities and Pharmacies

Gran Canaria is well-equipped with medical facilities, and pharmacies are plentiful. If you need any medication, look for a sign that says "Farmacia." Most pharmacists speak English and can assist you with common ailments or minor injuries. On one of my trips, I caught a cold and the local pharmacy in Puerto Rico was a lifesaver – they recommended the perfect over-the-counter meds to get me back on my feet in no time.

Staying Safe

Safety is always a priority, and while Gran Canaria is generally safe for tourists, here are some tips to keep you out of trouble.

1. Personal Belongings

Like any tourist destination, petty theft can happen. Keep your belongings close, especially in crowded places like markets or public transportation. I usually carry a small crossbody bag that I can keep in front of me and always lock my valuables in the hotel safe. In Las Palmas, I met a fellow traveler who had his wallet taken from his back pocket while on a crowded bus – so be cautious!

2. Safe Transportation

If you're renting a car, always lock the doors and don't leave valuables inside. The roads are generally good, but driving can be a bit hectic in the city centers. I found it easier to use public transportation or taxis in places like Las Palmas. The local buses are reliable and cover most of the island. Taxis are also a safe option – just ensure they use the meter.

3. Beach Safety

The beaches in Gran Canaria are stunning, but it's important to swim in designated areas and pay attention to the lifeguards' instructions. Some beaches have strong currents, so it's better to be safe and swim where it's monitored. One day at Playa del Inglés, the red flag was up indicating dangerous conditions, and I saw a few people get into trouble by ignoring it. Don't be that person!

4. Nightlife Precautions

Gran Canaria has a vibrant nightlife, especially in areas like Playa del Inglés and Maspalomas. While it's generally safe, always stick to well-lit areas and avoid walking alone late at night. If you're out enjoying the nightlife, keep an eye on your drink and don't accept drinks from strangers. I had a great time at a local bar in Maspalomas, but I always made sure to follow these basic precautions.

5. Hiking and Outdoor Activities

Gran Canaria offers fantastic hiking and outdoor activities. When heading out for an adventure, always let someone know your plans and estimated return time. Carry a map, a charged phone, and sufficient supplies. Once, I went hiking in the Barranco de Guayadeque and got a bit turned around – thankfully, I had my phone and a map, and I was able to find my way back without much hassle.

Emergency Contacts

Having a list of emergency contacts is a must when traveling. Here are some important numbers and addresses you should keep handy:

1. Emergency Services

Police, Fire, Ambulance: 112

This is the general emergency number for any situation. Operators usually speak English and can direct your call appropriately.

2. Medical Assistance

Hospital Insular de Gran Canaria

Address: Av. Marítima del Sur, s/n, 35016 Las Palmas de Gran Canaria, Las Palmas, Spain

Phone: +34 928 441 000

Hospital Doctor Negrín

Address: C/ Barranco de La Ballena, s/n, 35010 Las Palmas de Gran Canaria, Las Palmas, Spain

Phone: +34 928 450 000

3. Tourist Assistance

Tourist Information Office – Las Palmas

Address: Parque de Santa Catalina, s/n, 35007 Las Palmas de Gran Canaria, Las Palmas, Spain

Phone: +34 928 260 589

Tourist Information Office – Maspalomas

Address: Av. de Tirajana, 28, 35100 Maspalomas, Las Palmas, Spain

Phone: +34 928 720 035

4. Pharmacies

Farmacia Las Canteras

Address: Calle de Fernando Guanarteme, 60, 35010 Las Palmas de Gran Canaria, Las Palmas, Spain

Phone: +34 928 263 645

Farmacia Puerto Rico

Address: Avenida Tomas Roca Bosch, 35130 Puerto Rico, Las Palmas, Spain

Phone: +34 928 561 023

5. Embassies and Consulates

British Consulate Las Palmas

Address: Calle Luis Morote, 6, 3ª Planta, 35007 Las Palmas de Gran Canaria, Las Palmas, Spain

Phone: +34 928 267 774

German Consulate Las Palmas

Address: Calle Albareda, 3, 2º, 35007 Las Palmas de Gran Canaria, Las Palmas, Spain

Phone: +34 928 491 880

6. Local Contacts

Gran Canaria Tourist Board

Address: Av. de la Feria, 1, 35012 Las Palmas de Gran Canaria, Las Palmas, Spain

Phone: +34 928 219 600

Red Cross Gran Canaria

Address: C/ León y Castillo, 231, 35005 Las Palmas de Gran Canaria, Las Palmas, Spain

Phone: +34 928 296 000

Traveling is an adventure, and being prepared ensures it's a positive one. Gran Canaria is a wonderful place, filled with beautiful landscapes, rich culture, and friendly locals. By following these health and safety tips, you can fully enjoy your time on this magnificent island without any worries. Safe travels, and make the most of every moment in Gran Canaria!

Chapter 19

Language Tips for Travelers

Basic Phrases

When I first arrived in Gran Canaria, I quickly realized that while many people speak English, knowing some basic Spanish phrases can make your experience much smoother and more enjoyable. Here are a few key phrases that I found incredibly helpful:

Hola (Hello): A simple greeting that opens up conversations.

Buenos días (Good morning): A polite way to start your day.

Buenas tardes (Good afternoon): Used from noon until evening.

Buenas noches (Good night): For late evening greetings and goodbyes.

Por favor (Please): Essential for polite requests.

Gracias (Thank you): Always appreciated after any interaction.

De nada (You're welcome): A nice response when someone thanks you.

¿Cómo estás? (How are you?): A friendly way to ask about someone's well-being.

Bien, gracias (Fine, thank you): A common response to the above.

¿Dónde está...? (Where is...?): Very useful for asking directions.

¿Cuánto cuesta? (How much does it cost?): Handy for shopping and dining.

Lo siento (I'm sorry): Important for apologies.

Perdón (Excuse me): Useful for getting someone's attention or if you bump into someone.

Sí (Yes) and No (No): Basic responses you'll use frequently.

Knowing these phrases not only helped me navigate through daily interactions but also showed the locals that I was making an effort to respect their language and culture. Trust me, a little Spanish goes a long way!

Helpful Expressions

Beyond the basics, there are a few expressions that can come in handy and make your conversations more engaging. These phrases can help you handle various situations, from dining out to exploring the island.

¿Puede ayudarme? (Can you help me?): When you need assistance.

¿Habla inglés? (Do you speak English?): A polite way to inquire if someone can communicate in English.

No entiendo (I don't understand): Useful if you're struggling with the language.

¿Puede repetirlo, por favor? (Can you repeat that, please?): Helpful if you need someone to say something again.

¿Dónde puedo encontrar un taxi? (Where can I find a taxi?): Essential for transportation.

La cuenta, por favor (The bill, please): When you're ready to pay at a restaurant.

Una mesa para dos, por favor (A table for two, please): For dining out.

¿Tiene recomendaciones? (Do you have any recommendations?): Great for getting local tips on food, places to visit, etc.

Estoy perdido (I'm lost): If you need help finding your way.

¿Dónde está el baño? (Where is the bathroom?): Always a necessity!

Quisiera… (I would like…): Useful for ordering food or drinks.

Using these expressions made my interactions more fluid and natural. Whether I was asking for directions or trying new foods, these phrases bridged the gap between my limited Spanish and the locals' friendly assistance.

Language Resources

To make the most of my time in Gran Canaria, I relied on a few resources that helped me improve my

Spanish and communicate more effectively. Here are some tools and tips that I found invaluable:

Language Apps: Apps like Duolingo and Babbel were great for learning on the go. I would practice during my flights or while waiting in lines, picking up new words and phrases quickly.

Phrasebooks: Carrying a small Spanish phrasebook was a lifesaver. I used the "Lonely Planet Spanish Phrasebook & Dictionary," which was compact and easy to reference.

Local Classes: Taking a short Spanish course at a local language school can be a fun way to immerse yourself. I joined a beginner class at the Gran Canaria School of Languages (Calle Dr. Grau Bassas, 27, 35007 Las Palmas de Gran Canaria, Phone: +34 928 27 73 38), which offered intensive courses that fit my travel schedule.

Conversational Exchanges: I found a local language exchange group through Meetup. These informal gatherings were a fantastic way to practice Spanish with native speakers while they practiced their English. It also led to some wonderful friendships.

Listening and Watching: I started listening to Spanish music and watching Spanish shows with subtitles. This helped me get used to the rhythm and sounds of the language. "El Ministerio del Tiempo" became a favorite TV series of mine, and I enjoyed the music of artists like Pablo Alborán and Rosalía.

Flashcards: Using flashcard apps like Anki helped me memorize vocabulary efficiently. I would review these during downtime, reinforcing my learning daily.

Local Interactions: Engaging with locals was the best practice. I tried to speak Spanish whenever I could—at restaurants, shops, and even casual conversations at the beach. The locals were patient and appreciated my efforts, often correcting me gently and teaching me new words.

Tourist Information Centers: These centers often have bilingual staff who can help you with directions, recommendations, and any questions you might have. The main Tourist Information Office in Las Palmas (Calle Mayor de Triana, 93, 35002 Las Palmas de Gran Canaria, Phone: +34 928 33 88 84) was particularly helpful and provided maps and brochures in multiple languages.

By integrating these resources into my daily routine, I found that my confidence in speaking Spanish grew significantly. The more I practiced, the more natural it felt, and the more I could connect with the beautiful culture of Gran Canaria.

My Personal Experience

One of my most memorable experiences with the local language happened during a visit to a charming little tapas bar in Las Palmas. I was determined to order in Spanish and struck up a conversation with the bartender, Juan.

"Hola, ¿qué tal?" I greeted him with a smile.

"¡Hola! Muy bien, gracias. ¿Y tú?" he replied.

I managed to convey my interest in trying some local dishes, and he recommended a few specialties. "Quisiera probar el pulpo a la gallega y unas croquetas, por favor," I said, proud of my effort.

Juan nodded approvingly. "¡Perfecto! ¿Algo para beber?"

"Sí, una copa de vino tinto, por favor."

The interaction felt rewarding, and Juan appreciated my attempt to speak his language. He even took the time to explain each dish in detail, enhancing my dining experience. The pulpo a la gallega (Galician-style octopus) was delicious, and the croquetas were some of the best I've ever had. It was a small moment, but it made my trip feel more authentic and personal.

Later that evening, as I strolled back to my hotel, I reflected on how much these language interactions enriched my travel experience. Gran Canaria wasn't just a beautiful destination; it was a place where I could connect with people, learn new things, and immerse myself in a different culture. The effort I put into learning Spanish was more than worth it, and it opened doors to unforgettable experiences.

If you're planning a trip to Gran Canaria, I highly recommend taking some time to learn a bit of Spanish. It's a wonderful way to show respect for the local culture and enhance your overall travel experience. ¡Buena suerte y disfruta tu viaje! (Good luck and enjoy your trip!)

Chapter 20

Sustainable and Responsible Tourism

Eco-Friendly Practices

When I first set foot on Gran Canaria, I was struck by its natural beauty and diverse landscapes. From the lush greenery of the north to the arid, sun-drenched south, the island offers a remarkable variety of environments. As I spent more time here, I realized how crucial it is to protect this paradise for future generations. Here are some eco-friendly practices I've embraced and recommend to fellow travelers.

Choose Sustainable Accommodations

Opting for eco-friendly accommodations can make a big difference. During my stay, I found several hotels and guesthouses committed to sustainable practices. One such place is Finca Las Longueras (Calle de la Cruz, 35480 Agaete, Gran Canaria, Spain; +34 928 898 252), a charming rural hotel that uses solar energy, recycles waste, and supports local agriculture. Staying here not only provided a comfortable base but also the satisfaction of contributing to environmental conservation.

Reduce Plastic Use

Plastic pollution is a global issue, and Gran Canaria is no exception. To minimize my plastic footprint, I carried a reusable water bottle and shopping bags. Many local stores, like Verde Canario (Calle Cano 3, Las Palmas de Gran Canaria, +34 928 331 390), offer biodegradable or reusable options, making it easier to avoid single-use plastics.

Use Public Transport and Bikes

Gran Canaria's public transportation system is efficient and extensive, covering most tourist spots and local attractions. I frequently used the buses operated by Global (Estación de Guaguas San Telmo, Las Palmas de Gran Canaria; +34 928 252 630) to get around. For shorter distances, renting a bike was both fun and eco-friendly. Companies like Free Motion (Av. de Italia, 1, 35100 Playa del Inglés; +34 928 777 777) offer a variety of bikes for rent, allowing you to explore at your own pace while reducing carbon emissions.

Respect Natural Habitats

Gran Canaria is home to unique flora and fauna, some of which are endemic to the island. While hiking in natural parks like Parque Natural Tamadaba, I made sure to stay on marked trails and avoid disturbing wildlife. Guided tours, such as those offered by Rocky Adventure (Calle España, 13, 35100 Maspalomas; +34 928 763 819), provide valuable insights into the island's ecosystems and how to enjoy them responsibly.

Supporting Local Communities

Traveling sustainably also means supporting the local economy and communities. Gran Canaria's vibrant culture and warm hospitality are best experienced through its people.

Buy Local Products

One of my favorite experiences was visiting local markets and shops. The Mercado de Vegueta (Plaza del Mercado, s/n, 35001 Las Palmas de Gran Canaria) is a treasure trove of fresh produce, handmade crafts, and local delicacies. Here, I met artisans like Juan, who sells beautiful, handwoven baskets, and Maria, whose organic cheeses are simply divine. Buying directly from locals not only ensures quality but also supports their livelihoods.

Dine at Local Restaurants

Gran Canaria's culinary scene is rich and diverse, reflecting its history and cultural influences. I made it a point to eat at locally-owned restaurants rather than international chains. La Bodega de La Marea (Calle León y Castillo, 282, 35005 Las Palmas de Gran Canaria; +34 928 270 220) offers a fantastic selection of Canarian dishes made from locally-sourced ingredients. Their papas arrugadas with mojo sauce is a must-try! Dining here not only satisfied my taste buds but also supported local farmers and chefs.

Participate in Community Events

During my stay, I was fortunate to attend several local festivals and events. The Fiesta de La Rama in Agaete is a vibrant celebration where locals dance and offer branches to the sea as a tribute to their ancestors. Participating in such events deepened my connection to the culture and contributed to the community. Check with the local tourist office for a calendar of events and join in whenever you can.

Minimizing Your Footprint

Being mindful of our impact on the environment is crucial, especially in a fragile ecosystem like Gran Canaria. Here are some practical steps I took to minimize my footprint while enjoying my stay.

Conserve Water and Energy

Water is a precious resource on the island. Simple actions like taking shorter showers, reusing towels, and turning off taps while brushing teeth can significantly reduce water consumption. Many hotels have energy-saving initiatives, such as key card systems that control the room's power. Embracing these practices was an easy yet effective way to minimize my environmental impact.

Dispose of Waste Properly

Gran Canaria has a robust recycling system, and I made sure to separate my waste accordingly. Many accommodations and public areas provide clearly labeled bins for different types of waste. Composting organic waste is also an option in some rural areas. When hiking or spending time outdoors, I always carried a small bag to collect my trash and disposed of it properly.

Choose Sustainable Activities

Instead of motorized tours, I opted for eco-friendly activities. Kayaking with Canary Wave (Calle Fragata, 3, 35100 Maspalomas; +34 928 769 230) was a highlight, offering a unique perspective of the coastline without the noise and pollution of motorboats. Similarly, snorkeling and diving with eco-conscious operators like Davy Jones Diving (Calle Luján Pérez, 13, 35100 Arinaga; +34 928 173 093) allowed me to explore the underwater world responsibly.

Educate Yourself and Others

One of the most impactful things we can do as travelers is to educate ourselves and share our knowledge. I took the time to learn about Gran Canaria's environmental challenges and conservation efforts by visiting places like the Jardín Botánico Canario Viera y Clavijo (Carretera del Centro, Km 7, 35017 Las Palmas de Gran Canaria; +34 928 219 580). This botanical garden showcases the island's diverse plant life and highlights the importance of conservation. Sharing these experiences with fellow travelers and friends helps spread awareness and encourages more people to travel responsibly.

In conclusion, traveling sustainably and responsibly in Gran Canaria enriched my experience in countless ways. By adopting eco-friendly practices, supporting local communities, and minimizing my footprint, I was able to enjoy the island's natural beauty and vibrant culture while contributing to its preservation.

I encourage every traveler to embrace these principles, ensuring that Gran Canaria remains a paradise for future generations to enjoy.

Appendix

Useful Contacts

When traveling to Gran Canaria, it's always good to have some essential contacts handy. Here are a few that I found extremely useful during my visit:

Emergency Services (Police, Fire, Ambulance): Dial 112

Tourist Information Center: Plaza de España, Las Palmas de Gran Canaria; +34 928 219 600

Hospital Universitario de Gran Canaria Dr. Negrín: Barranco de la Ballena, s/n, 35010 Las Palmas de Gran Canaria; +34 928 450 000

Consulate General of the United States: Calle Juan de Quesada, 35001 Las Palmas de Gran Canaria; +34 928 221 050

Consulate of the United Kingdom: Plaza de la Victoria, 8, 35005 Las Palmas de Gran Canaria; +34 928 262 508

Map of Gran Canaria

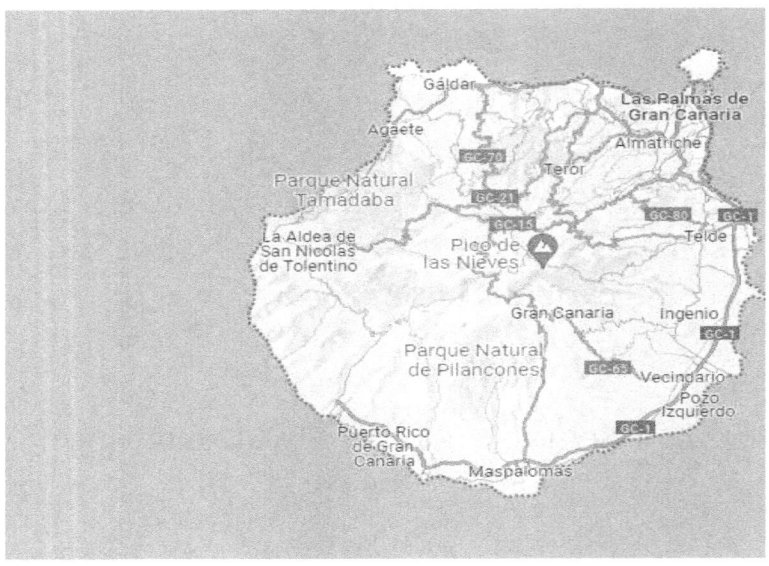

https://maps.app.goo.gl/rmEDxx1kKRMt7kQA6

SCAN THE IMAGE/QR CODE WITH YOUR PHONE TO GET THE LOCATIONS IN REAL

TIME.

Map of Things to do in Gran Canaria

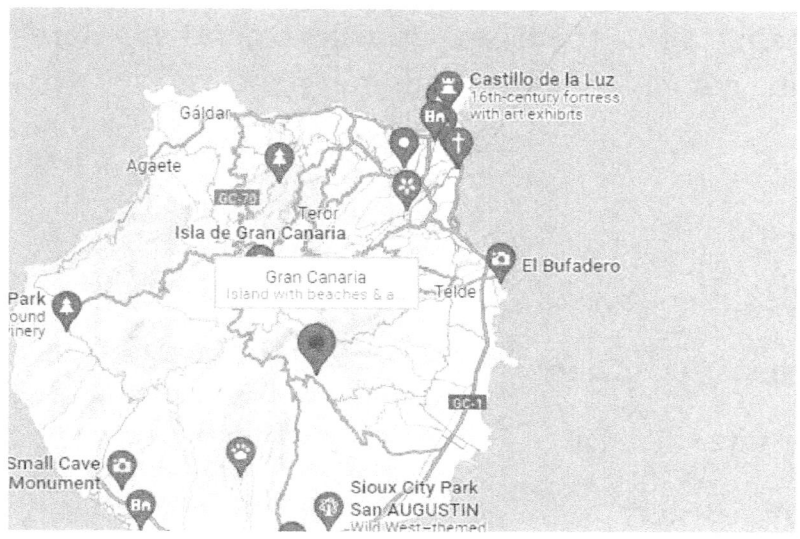

https://www.google.de/maps/search/things+to+do+in+Gran+Canaria/@27.9582861,-15.9261064,10z/data=!3m1!4b1?entry=ttu

SCAN THE IMAGE/QR CODE WITH YOUR PHONE TO GET THE LOCATIONS IN REAL TIME.

Glossary: Local Terms

Understanding a few local terms can go a long way in making your travel experience smoother. Here are some commonly used terms and phrases:

Hola: Hello

Adiós: Goodbye

Gracias: Thank you

Por favor: Please

Playa: Beach

Montaña: Mountain

Museo: Museum

Restaurante: Restaurant

Applications and Useful Resources

Technology can be a great travel companion. Here are some apps and resources that I found particularly helpful:

Google Maps: For navigation and exploring local attractions

Duolingo: To brush up on Spanish phrases

TripAdvisor: For reviews and recommendations

Rome2Rio: For planning transportation routes

XE Currency: For currency conversion

Addresses and Locations of Popular Accommodations

Finding the right place to stay is crucial. Here are some top accommodations with their addresses:

Hotel Santa Catalina: Calle León y Castillo, 227, 35005 Las Palmas de Gran Canaria; +34 928 243 040

Hotel Riu Palace Meloneras: Calle Mar Mediterráneo, 1, 35100 Meloneras; +34 928 142 000

Hotel Cordial Mogán Playa: Avenida Los Marrero, 2, 35138 Puerto de Mogán; +34 928 724 100

Addresses and Locations of Popular Restaurants and Cafés

Gran Canaria boasts a vibrant culinary scene. Here are some restaurants and cafés I recommend:

Restaurante La Aquarela: Barranco de la Verga, s/n, 35120 Arguineguín; +34 928 735 891

El Churrasco: Calle León y Castillo, 227, 35005 Las Palmas de Gran Canaria; +34 928 277 834

Café Regina: Calle Mayor de Triana, 44, 35002 Las Palmas de Gran Canaria; +34 928 366 108

Addresses and Locations of Popular Bars and Clubs

For a taste of the nightlife, check out these popular spots:

La Azotea de Benito: Calle Triana, 33, 35002 Las Palmas de Gran Canaria; +34 928 369 292

Fortuni: Calle Joaquín Costa, 1, 35007 Las Palmas de Gran Canaria; +34 928 270 182

El Tendedero de Catalina: Calle Cano, 5, 35002 Las Palmas de Gran Canaria; +34 928 433 775

Addresses and Locations of Top Attractions

Gran Canaria is rich in attractions. Here are some must-visit spots with their addresses:

Roque Nublo: Near Tejeda, Gran Canaria

Palmitos Park: Barranco de Los Palmitos, s/n, 35109 Maspalomas; +34 928 797 070

Vegueta: Historic district in Las Palmas de Gran Canaria

Maspalomas Dunes: Near Playa del Inglés, Gran Canaria

Cueva Pintada Museum and Archaeological Park: Calle Audiencia, 2, 35460 Gáldar; +34 928 895 746

This appendix should help you navigate and enjoy Gran Canaria with ease, ensuring you have a fulfilling and enjoyable stay on this beautiful island.

Photo Attributions

https://www.freepik.com/free-vector/worker-with-doubts_834551.htm#fromView=search&page=2&position=37&uuid=8a977674-9b27-4474-9948-088924cb904a

Printed in Great Britain
by Amazon